Y0-BYH-568

MARRIAGE OF THE MIND

∇ ∇ ∇

Marriage of the Mind
Processes of Insight and Integration

by
George F. Buletza, Ph.D.

AMORC

©1997, Supreme Grand Lodge of the Ancient &
Mystical Order Rosae Crucis.

Published by the Grand Lodge of the
English Language Jurisdiction, AMORC, Inc.

©1997 by Supreme Grand Lodge of AMORC, Inc.
All Rights Reserved

ISBN 0-912057-94-7

©1997, Supreme Grand Lodge of the Ancient & Mystical Order Rosae Crucis
Published by the Grand Lodge of the English Language Jurisdication,
AMORC, Inc.

Library of Congress Catalog Card No.: 97-066324

No part of this publication may be reproduced, stored in a retrieval system, or transmitted, in any form
or by any means, electronic, mechanical, photocopying, recording, or otherwise, without prior written
permission of the publisher.

Cover Art: © 1997, Supreme Grand Lodge of the Ancient &
Mystical Order Rosae Crucis

10 9 8 7 6 5 4 3 2 1

Printed and bound in U.S.A.

DEDICATION

▼

TO THE GOD OF OUR HEARTS
AND REALIZATION

▼

*This book is dedicated to You who gave us the Rose and the Cross that
we might know Mastery in Self. You have given us the means to
let go of all impediments to Self-Mastery, the means to be as
we are created to be: a full, integrated, and coherent
expression of the unity and wholeness that is the
Cosmic. This book is dedicated to You, the
Divine Essence that is the Heart of
each one of us.*

▼

The Rosicrucian Library

Other volumes will be added from time to time.
Write for complete catalogue. See address on last page.

CONTENTS

(Continued on next page)

APPENDICES

LIST OF ILLUSTRATIONS

FIGURES

(Continued on next page)

TABLES

PREFACE

Youthful inner direction led me to a fascination with the workings of the mind and nervous system. I wanted to know how the mind worked and how it could be used. If it were true that we only use ten percent of our brain, then I wanted to learn and to assist others in learning how to use more of the total mental power that we possess. It was obvious that my future work lay in being prepared in the "hard" sciences, neuroanatomy, neurocytology, and neurochemistry. Graduate studies and post-doctoral work became more and more technical and specialized. I began to wonder about the fulfillment of my life purpose. Then, unexpectedly, the opportunity to undertake the kind of investigations into the nature of self that I was most interested in presented itself.

I became a member of the Rosicrucian Order, AMORC (The Ancient Mystical Order Rosae Crucis), in 1961. During the first few months of my early studies both at Ohio Wesleyan University in Delaware, Ohio, and with the Rosicrucian Order, AMORC, little about the Order was known to me except through advertisements promising a scientific and esoteric method of study. Following an inner urge, it was clear to me that Rosicrucian studies would provide me with practical strategies for directly dealing with what I perceived to be problematic and important. The events of the time, my early studies and experiences, all appealed to my penchant for inner direction.

For me, joining the Order was a homecoming. Here were people who approached life philosophically and esoterically, the way I wanted to. As a group they talked about atomic theory and then reflected upon its personal significance. They investigated the mind and then reflected upon its importance to everyday life.

Rosicrucian studies provided me with an outline or su-, perstructure upon which I could fit all the course work required in college. And this proved to be the case throughout graduate school at the University of California at Berkeley, where I received my Ph.D., and in my post-doctoral research work at Stanford University Medical School. Moreover, these practical approaches and techniques provided methods for verifying personal goals and the meaning life had for me. My first experiences with these Rosicrucian teachings provided me with practical strategies for directly dealing with life's opportunities and what I perceived as terrible problems.

In the summer of 1975 the Rosicrucian Order reinstituted a research program started some fifty years before by the first Imperator in North America, Dr. H. Spencer Lewis. Since I served on the summer faculty of Rose-Croix University, served as a member of AMORC's International Research Council, and as Master of Oakland Lodge, it was natural that I be asked to consult in the formation of a new research program. Part-time consulting grew into full-time directing of laboratories, personnel, and investigations. For twelve years, *Mindquest*, a monthly report and article dealing with our research, was published in the *Rosicrucian Digest* and then translated and published in eight languages.

The subject that was central to the many investigations made in the AMORC research facilities at Rosicrucian Park and in the laboratories of members of the International Research Council was a process of thought leading to insight, integration, and new expressions of creativity.

Through this book, I am grateful for the opportunity to share with you my enthusiasm for a way of experiencing life and self whose origins can be found in antiquity.

* * *

Many people contributed to the creation of this book. The ideas and processes explored here were also entertained, experienced, and explored in antiquity and evolved over many centuries. In our present cycle of experience these ideas were once again investigated, promulgated, and shared by the officers, employees, and members of AMORC. Research that greatly contributed to this body of work was conducted by a fine team of AMORC scientists and other staff researchers, both at Rosicrucian Park and throughout the world. A special acknowledgment goes to AMORC researchers Michael Bukay, Sandra Huff, June Schaa, Christine Van Dorn, and Dr. Onslow Wilson.

Personally, I also received the benefit of tutelage from many teachers. Foremost of these were Dr. Marian E. Smith at Stanford University Medical School and the VA Hospital in Palo Alto; Dr. Wilbur B. Quay, of the University of California, at Berkeley; and Dr. Theodore R. Atkins at Clemson University. Dr. Bernice Zamora and Madge Doss edited the original manuscript. In addition, many friends also made suggestions, read chapters for me, inserted tables and figures. These supportive friends included Carmen and Juan Alvarez, Francoise Beaudoin, Roberta Ellarae, Pall Grondal,

Tim Sika, Linda Stanley, Jacqueline and Robert Vickery. The additional love and assistance of many colleagues, friends, and loved ones throughout the world resulted in the gift, to me, of this book.

CHAPTER 1

BEGINNINGS

Our physical senses and objective consciousness give to the outer world a sense of substantiality and reality. Some of us, however, also dream of *first causes*. This is the very essence of metaphysics. Many people have an inner yearning for meaning and significance, for the eternal, the beautiful, the true. Our feelings, emotions, and sentiments of love, peace, and joy can seem formless, and yet these qualities of our experience can be as much a part of our consciousness as the outer world we see, hear, touch, taste, and smell. Our subjective, inner experiences, however, can appear to be more vague and intangible than our more concrete and objective ones.

Although some of us may be unaware of it, we all constantly search for the bond between the two worlds, the infinite and the finite, or the spiritual and the material. Even in the ancient world, there were people who noticed that they were so constituted as to perceive two worlds. Some ancient philosophers and medieval alchemists termed this bonding or union of objective and imaginative faculties the *Mystical Marriage*, the *Mysterium Coniunctionis*, or what some today call the *Marriage of the Mind.* This mystical marriage is a universal pattern lying deep within ourselves, being essential to the experience and expression of what we actually are. This Marriage of the Mind is one of the most important subjects we can choose to investigate while on the path leading to Mastery in Self.

Ancient myths tell us that the chosen path which leads to the Mystical Marriage is important in and of itself. The *Chymical Wedding of Christian Rosenkreutz* tells us that there are four paths to choose from as we journey to the Marriage Feast. The First Way is short, but filled with danger, fearful dragons, birds of prey, steep ascents, precipices, and the many obstacles and pitfalls found with trial-and-error approaches in life. Those who arrive at the Marriage Feast by this route are filled with attitudes and feelings of conceit, self-importance, and *hubris*—that is, what the ancient Greeks were referring to as *overweening pride*. The people who succeed on this first way feel that their great accomplishments and achievements are solely due to their own efforts; nothing is simply given to them as a gift of life. Unfortunately, their pride and arrogance also prevents them from receiving the fruits of illumination and insight, which are the gifts of the Chymical Marriage.

Those who chose the long, easy, meandering path, the Second Way, did not show up at the feast before the story ended. Presumably, they were still aimlessly drifting through life when the tale was over. We might hope, however, that maybe they would make it for the next telling of the story.

The Third Way was one meant for spirits. Christian Rosenkreutz felt that this way was unfit for himself, or for people like us. Some people in mystical pursuits choose such a way, and become lost in purple and pastel fantasies that have little connection to objective realms of consciousness. Certain ancient myths speak of time spent in such a fairyland reverie, before the hero or heroine realize the mistake and choose to break the spell and return to the world. In the Arthurian romances, Morgan Le Fay spent many weeks in such a fairyland before regaining her senses and returning to Camelot and her duties in Avalon.

The fourth way was simply called the Royal Road. To enter upon this path one had to recognize that he or she had been one of the chosen. Even Christian Rosenkreutz found such a choosing to be intimidating. Yet, judging himself to be unworthy or not, he still found himself walking on this Royal Road because, enraptured, he had followed a small, white bird (traditionally, a small, white bird represents innocence and intuition). This unlikely method of his election to the Royal Road caused Christian Rosenkreutz to doubt his worthiness. While still doubtful, he proceeded, discovering that on this fourth way questions were asked of him and gifts were given by the Gatekeepers of the way. He did not arrive at the feast by means of his ability alone. He arrived at the feast having shared his life and past experiences and having allowed them to be wedded to the Royal Gifts that were given along the way.

Since ancient times, people have had intuitions about the two sides of a divided human nature, sometimes expressed as *Eros* and *Logos*, heart and mind, the right-hand way and the left-hand way. Even in our most objective and rational moments we can feel a counterweight within: the vague and undefinable aspects of our imagination and subconscious. These intuitions and creative urges usually are the province of poets, philosophers, and mystics, rather than the province of the common-sense view of the man of science and worldly affairs. However, the facts of recent neurological and psychological investigations on hemispheric functioning are now moving the views of science closer to that of the poets and mystics. Modern research indicates that there are two basic ways of knowing, based upon differences in the functioning of our two cerebral hemispheres. Hence, the purpose of this book is our personal realization of our unity and oneness of consciousness. In such a wholeness, we can know the "marriage" of these two ways of experiencing life.

In research conducted by Rosicrucians, we have found that we can all be seeking insight and illumination—the fruits of the Mystical Marriage. Yet, creative insight often seems to have a will of its own. We can spend hours, days, or even months trying to solve a problem with little apparent success. Then, suddenly, without mental effort, the solution flashes across the screen of our consciousness, accompanied by feelings of "aha!," certainty and joy. In order to study in the laboratory this natural process of insight experience, a system of questions was devised. Rather than only approaching this subject in an abstract way, you may enjoy experiencing this thought process for yourself.

In the next chapter there are a series of questions designed to direct you through objective, formative, and symbolic states of consciousness. As many Rosicrucian students have done, you may also wish to choose to work with a candle flame as a point of concentration for answering these questions for yourself, and then you will be able to compare your answers with composite answers drawn from the responses of many of these students. This comparison will assist you in assessing whether your answers are specific and addressed to the questions asked. Note your body sensations or feelings as you pass from one state of consciousness to another. When you are objectively describing something, do you *feel* the same as when you are describing how something works? What are your body sensations as you ask yourself what meaning can this something hold for you? What can you learn about yourself from these changes in feeling and mood? Could this have anything to do with your realization of your Mastery in Self?

CHAPTER 2

CREATING SYMBOLS OF TRANSFORMATION

The creative process is dual in nature. It involves both an active *doing* and a receptive *not-doing*. The doing part requires concentration, study, and analysis. Not-doing involves relaxing the objective mind so that there results a release of the Inner Self's powers. At a subconscious level, disjointed thoughts shift and realign themselves, and a solution or inspiration spontaneously appears. In AMORC's research facilities we wondered if this process of creative insight and the likelihood of illumination could be facilitated and directed. We asked ourselves whether the principles contained in the Thought Process (utilizing the principles and techniques of Concentration, Contemplation, Meditation, and Assumption) could be used to join together doing and not-doing, conscious and subconscious activities, so that we could improve our ability to master ourselves and creatively direct the forces of nature.

To study the natural process of insight in the laboratory, we used a system of questions based on Rosicrucian principles and techniques. We observed that this system of questions could indeed guide a person through the various learning stages leading to an insight experience. To start the process, subjects first chose an object of interest on which to concentrate. They then answered a series of questions about the object of concentration. Many subjects chose a burning flame. The following summary demonstrates how a subject concentrates by using a candle flame and this process. The summary is a composite drawn from the responses of many subjects.

CONCENTRATION

Question: How would you objectively describe the candle flame in terms of your five physical senses?

Answer: People pointed out that, "the flame is blue at the base and gradually merges into bright yellow at the tip." Others said, "I see an aura around the flame." "Melted wax drips down the side of the candle and smoke rises from the flame." "The wick is black with a red spot on its tip." "As the flame burns the candle gets smaller."

"The flame is hot to touch yet I can pass my finger quickly through the flame without being burned." "I can smell a slight odor of the burning candle but I do not hear nor taste the flame."

Question: What does fire do? How does fire affect your life?

Answer: Responses to this question included, "Fire gives light and warmth." "One fire can start other fires thereby multiplying its light and warmth." "I use fire to cook food and heat my home." "My car runs by burning gasoline." "The metal in my car was smelted with fire." "Fire is the basis of industry." "The Sun and stars are fire. All life on earth is fueled by Sun-fire. All chemical elements were born in the furnace of stars." "If fire did not exist, neither would I in my present form."

CONTEMPLATION

Question: You have observed fire and you know what fire does. How does it do this? Why is it capable of doing this? In other words, what is the mechanism of action by which fire accomplishes what it does?

Answer: In contemplating an answer to this question, many people reported a shift in consciousness from that of concentration. One person remarked, "When hot enough, an object bursts into flame. The flame combines with oxygen and produces light, heat, and new chemicals." Others added, "The flame ignites other objects by raising their vibratory rate so that they, too, combine with oxygen." "When the oxygen is depleted or the fuel expended, the fire dies."

"The Sun-fire does not use oxygen. Hydrogen is converted to helium by a process of nuclear fusion. Eventually the Sun will consume itself. Its spent atoms will gradually coalesce and become building blocks for newer, evolving stars."

Question: How does the mechanism of fire which you have just described operate in and through you? Analogously, how are you similar to fire?

Answer: For many people this question evoked a sense of poetry, analogy, and metaphor. People stated that, "Like fire, my body consumes fuel and produces heat." "My thoughts radiate light which can help others along the path to understanding." "Each fire I set in the mind of others multiplies the light given to me." "When I die my soul-fire will continue to burn, and like the stars, I will be reborn in new form."

MEDITATION

Question: What is the meaning of the fire principle? What law is being illustrated?

Answer: Many begin to feel excitement when dealing with meaning and significance. Observations included, "The flowing, growing, expanding nature of the flame is a symbol of life." "By its association with body heat, fire symbolizes good health and also represents a wild craving for nourishment (the all-consuming fire)." "Both fire and life feed upon other lives in order to keep alive." "Fire is an alchemical element which operates in the center of things as a unifying, stabilizing factor." "Fire is related to the Sun, allied with central control and superiority."

"The fire principle is the seed which is reproduced in each successive life. As a mediator between forms which vanish and forms being created, fire is a symbol of transformation and regeneration." It is also an "agent of transmutation since all things derive from and return to fire."

Most symbols of life are also symbols of death. This is so because both life and death are conditions of change and

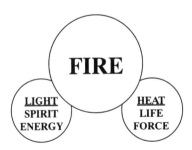

Fig. 1. *One subject's representation of the duality of fire.*

transition. Thus, "... fire is also a destroyer." The dualistic symbolism denotes both physical destruction and determination of spirit. "Fire is an image of energy which may be found at the level of animal passion as well as on the plane of psychic strength." One may give oneself up to the fire, simply use the fire for comfort, or steal the fire like Prometheus. However approached, it must be remembered that "fire is ultra-life." To pass through fire is symbolic of transcending the human condition.

In dealing with a candle flame, some people dealt with the nature of fire and others with light. For instance, some people pointed out that "Light is spirit. Spirit energy is recognizable by its luminous intensity. Its whiteness alludes to a synthesis of all." Light is also "... the creative force, cosmic energy emanating in seven colors." To become illumined with fire and light is to become aware of the light and, thus, of one's spiritual strength. (For a more detailed explanation of this process of Concentration, Contemplation, and Meditation, please see Appendix 1.)

ASSUMPTION

Question: In your imagination paint a nonverbal picture which illustrates your ideas about the meaning of this principle of fire. If you were to become the symbol of fire in your picture, what might you experience? Do not "control" your visualization, but simply observe what surprises occur.

Answer: The experience of being a symbol in our mind can be powerful and lead to the transformation of previous attitudes and outlooks in the world. As some people shared, "I become the fire and am surprised that there is no sense of heat. I extend tongues of flame and consume and purify objects around me."

"I take a problem and draw it into the fire of my Inner Self, burn away the outer trappings, and see the principle at the problem's core. I now project the principle out into the external world and give it new clothing and application." "By assuming that I am the fire I discover that I can be an agent of transmutation. Anything, not just problems, can be drawn into the fire, reduced to its essence, and projected back into the world in a purer form."

"I discover that as fire I must be careful not to burn other people but as I watch they, too, become fire. I combine with the fires of many people to form one big fire." "I experience the whole Earth united as a spiritual fire."

"As fire I enter into water. The water is very dark and black. I radiate light but I can no longer see the light I am radiating. I continue to radiate. The more I radiate the more the darkness of the water seems to close in on me. I fight this at first and then I let it happen. The dark water comes into my center, but then it is transmuted and is simultaneously radiated outward as fire and light. Simultaneously, the water flows into our center and flows outward as light. The seeming duality is all one, loving motion. Soon the waters are consumed and out of the puddle that is left rises a large golden globe. It is golden, but like an opal, shines with all the colors of the rainbow. As I enter the globe, I rediscover the dark water and at the center a star of fire and light. It is very difficult to relate in words the power and profound insight of this experience. The duality that resolves into one flow applies to everything!"

* * *

Descriptions as given here do not have as much meaning for the individual reader as having the actual insight experience for oneself. *Talking* about mystical experience does not equal *having* a mystical experience. The reader may wish to try several experiments such as the one outlined here. Concentration, contemplation, and meditation on water, air, or objects found in everyday experience (even paper clips, rubber bands, and pencils) have yielded surprising insights to research participants. The symbols and insights you discover are only limited by the limits you yourself put on your imagination.

Insight itself is a result of a unification of many thought processes, including the active and passive stages of concentration, contemplation, and meditation. This research program demonstrated that insight can be encouraged by the application of the aforementioned Rosicrucian principles and techniques. In the laboratory, physiological measurements taken during the various stages leading to insight resulted in observations of increasing parasympathetic activation or relaxation. Brain waves moved from high amplitude beta waves during concentration to low amplitude alpha and theta waves in meditation. During the experience of assumption where subjects imaginatively experienced what it might be like if they were the symbol in their picture, brain waves were flat from 1.5 to 40 Hertz on both sides of the brain. Nonetheless, subjects reported active experiences and surprising insights during this period. These studies are of great importance to the student, for with insight we can learn Mastery in Self and guidance of the forces of nature.

Fig. 2. *One subject's representation of the marriage of fire and water.*

CHAPTER 3

THOUGHT AS EXPERIENCE

PROCESS FOR THINKING TOGETHER

The word *thinking* is used so indiscriminately that it has lost precise meaning. It is commonly used to describe any process in the mental realm, frequently being used and confused with such words as *formulating, visualizing, considering, contemplating, reasoning, imagining, dreaming,* and so on. But regardless of how the term is used, thinking is normally associated with mental processes occurring within each individual mind. Apart from attention given to the sensorial perceived world, we also give attention to the processes of the mental world, to the parade of word forms and structures, and to our picture images and mental maps. What is commonly called *thinking* permits this mental world to exist.

Of course, individual minds can be linked together by their choosing to hold common thoughts, a sort of "metabolic" product of individual thinking processes. Today, thoughts are stored, transferred, and manipulated by such mental "prostheses" as books, computers, and television. The written and spoken word, and the pictured thought commonly expressed and shared, link together individual minds into groups and into ever larger organizations. Although common thoughts link minds into chains of being, the process of thinking still remains separate and self-contained within each individual mind. Each mind thinks apart. However, on matters of information and judgment it is generally accepted that "two heads are better than one." Indeed, when new ideas and approaches are being looked for, the more heads the better. Consequently, many minds are asked to participate on juries and referendums.

Modern research both supports and denies this view. When IQ tests made up of multiple-choice questions are administered to a group, an average IQ score is readily obtained. But if the plurality preference for each question is recorded and added together, to obtain the group's aggregate answers to each question (the collective knowledge as determined by referendum) the group's aggregate IQ score for all the questions is well above the group average, usually by as much as thirty points. Thus, any given question tends to be answered correctly by the majority. When the aggregating method is applied to the group's higher IQ scorers, the resulting aggregate group score is even more impressive. It can amount to as much as thirty points higher than that of its highest scoring member!

Dr. Norman Dalkey of UCLA (the originator of aggregate IQ scoring) and Dr. Arthur Jensen of the University of

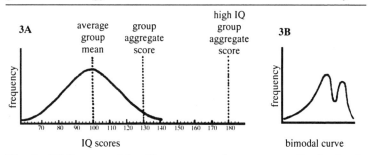

Fig. 3. *IQ Scores.* 3A. *Group mean of an average distribution in comparison to group aggregate scores.* 3B. *A bimodal curve.*

California at Berkeley have pointed out that there are logical reasons for cumulative intellectual power. On a difficult multiple-choice question most of the answers, being guesses, are spread more or less equally across all possible answers. This spread forms a normal distribution or a bell curve (see Fig. 3 A). However, those who really know the correct answers produce a *modal hump* (see Fig. 3 B). Their plurality vote would dictate the correct answer.

Minds linked together can act synergistically (for mutual benefit), yet in many groups and organizations individual minds are bound fast by the links in the chain. Indeed, in some groups synergism operates in reverse, the whole becomes less than the sum of its parts, not more. One reason for anti-synergistic thinking is group pressure for immediate convergence of thought. Face-to-face group discussions can quickly narrow the range of disagreement bringing about quick agreement on a wrong answer.

In group discussions a bias is often developed toward the most vocal segment of the group, with all members not having an equal chance to play an active role in determining judgments, forecasts, and decisions. This can be as true in community and business meetings as in structured stratagems such as symposia and brainstorming. Covering the blackboards with volunteered alternatives but without anonymity can be no more productive than "open" discussion, because this allows spoken error and bias to seep into generalized group assumptions without leaving any telltale trace on the record. For group discussions to be effective every member participates equally and every thought and idea offered is likewise treated equally and without bias.

Humility and open-minded group behavior may be a quality we are still striving to attain as a norm. In his book, *Victims of Groupthink*, Yale psychologist Dr. Irving Janis reports a surprisingly rigid adherence to group norms as well as unexpected pressures toward uniformity in otherwise highly intelligent groups. Committee group behavior was marked by illusions of invulnerability, arrogance, group loyalty, and illusions of unanimity and uniformity based on the fallacy that silence means consent. They collectively rationalized away suggestions that decisions be reconsidered, and self-appointed "mind-guards" emerged to shield the group from any information that might have shattered its complacency about the rightness of its decisions.

Is conformity a necessary product of groupthink? Is it possible to make intelligent, creative group decisions for the universal good, untrammeled by conformist pressures or the stresses of idiosyncratic thinking and emotion? "Perhaps," suggests Dr. John Calhoun of NIMH (National Institute of Mental Health), "if we were intelligent enough to develop a 'social brain' and then use it to its fullest potential." To do so, we might begin by seeing ourselves as if we were the individual neurons (brain cells) of a group mind. In other words, the individual mind of man might be used as an intuitive and logical model for society (see Fig. 4).

Such an evolved social brain would require a sensing system to scan the universe of concepts, ideas, philosophies, purposes, and functions, and it would require an imagining system to develop a continuous creative anthology and synthesis. Finally, an appreciative system would be required to discriminate, evaluate, and condense the group-generated

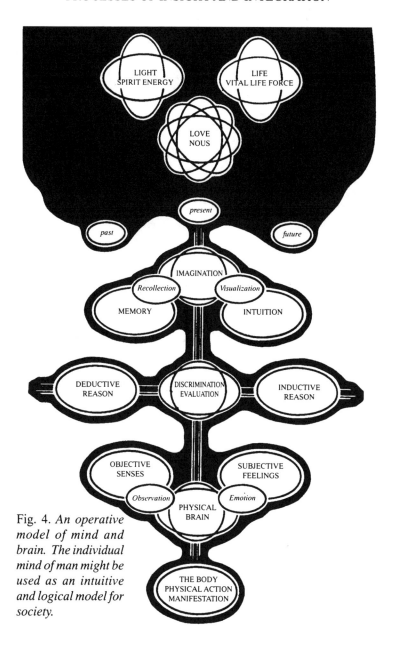

Fig. 4. *An operative model of mind and brain. The individual mind of man might be used as an intuitive and logical model for society.*

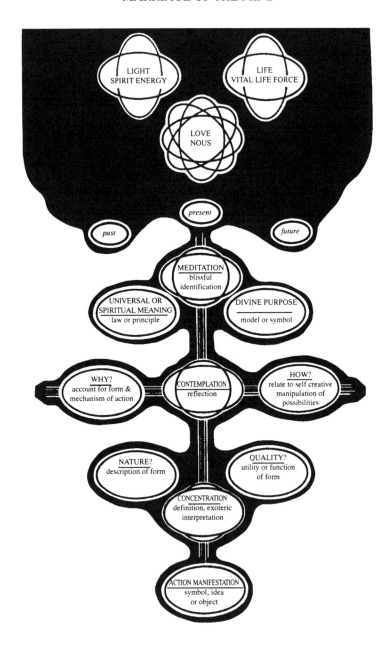

ideas into group-validated principles and ideals. Each member would become a unit in a mind greater than itself. Each member would not only share in the thoughts produced within the group, but would be a participant in a group thinking process.

The neurosciences teach that in the brain cortex each neuron is a self-contained, individual cellular unit. Each works silently and efficiently to add its part to the whole of thought. A single thought is a vibratory waveform that encompasses the entire cortex, being the product of the community of neurons working together. Impulses and messages originating in the lower brain centers are constantly integrated and evaluated in ever higher centers until finally impressions and thoughts burst forth in full awareness on the surface of the mind.

If such occupation and facilitation of ideas are to be accomplished in a social brain, then a method must be devised to transcend the influence of the kind of tyrannical group pressures revealed by Dr. Janis. A possible method is intimated by the aggregate scored IQ test wherein responses

---

⇦ Fig. 5. *An operative model of meditation. You may wish to use this model in composing your response for the Masterthoughts experiment. Begin concentrating by objectively definining the nature and use of* thought. *When you try to account for why* thought *works and how it operates within you, you may immediately note a shift in your inner state of consciousness. See if you feel differently when you objectively* define *in comparison to when you ask* why. *Many will again feel another shift as they examine the universal meaning of* thought *and when they ask to receive a universal symbol or picture which will unify all of their ideas and observations concerning* thought. *Concentration-contemplation-meditation is an orderly and holistic process of study leading to that knowledge and wisdom permeating mystic experience.*

are independently written out by each member of the group. With the written response the least talkative member is elevated to the same operational plane as the most garrulous. With a social brain, then, unbiased facilitation may be effected by having each member anonymously submit written responses, by having an unbiased jury review, and then by reporting the results back to the group. The freshly assimilated knowledge is then further refined through another round or two of the same silent procedure.

Will such a utopian model for a group mind really work? Can the thinking processes of individual minds be synthesized into the operations of a greater mind? Thinking together, can we produce practical, beneficial, and holistic results? We can experiment. Let us think together.

In 1977 each reader of Mindquest was invited to submit a concise, written response to the following three-part question: (1) What is thought?; (2) How does thought relate to man?; (3) Does thought have a universal purpose? Imagine a universal symbol which encompasses all of your ideas concerning thought.

THE NATURE OF THOUGHT

Over 400 Mindquest readers throughout the world submitted their ideas concerning the nature, use, and purpose of thought. A panel of ten people then reviewed the submitted ideas and each panel member wrote a synopsis. The AMORC Research Staff synthesized the synopses for presentation as a series of Mindquest reports.

From these reports it was obvious to the Rosicrucian scientists responsible for the Mindquest program that thinking involves emotion, reason, memory, intuition, and imagination, as well as the five senses. What also could be seen is that there is a basic element shared by objective, formative, and symbolic thinking. At each level of thought, *images* are used. Images are used to recollect, to create or receive new insight, to analyze, reason, evaluate, and observe. Thoughts constantly transform, moving, changing shape, and coalescing. Thoughts can be sustained, focused, and projected with suggestion and visualization in such processes as meditation, dream, prayer, and ritual. Some images even trigger the transformation of other images.

The movement of thought through consciousness can occur spontaneously or it can be directed at will. Whether directed or not, thoughts attract, channel, and give form to energy. Thought can be transmitted over a distance as in telepathy, and directed toward the ordering of movement in external objects. Recent experiments investigating psychokinesis have suggested that the emanative power of controlled thought can produce molecular changes in water, accelerate growth and regenerative processes in plants and animals, and cause objects to move as if propelled by some mysterious force. According to these views, thought would appear to have a concrete character, perhaps affirming the old adage that "thoughts are things," and as one contributor poetically adds:

Thoughts are free, for they are living things. The closer they dwell with truth, the greater the life-power flowing through them. Take care, for these living thoughts, these gentle seed of winged-life, for they are our children who will be our parents in the next rebirth.

Most participants who answered the question, "What is thought?" fell into two categories. One group (see Table 1) indicated that thought is a product of human consciousness and occurs as a person interacts with the environment. The other group (see Table 2) indicated that thought is the essence of all that exists within the Divine Mind.

In these tables the definitions of thought were classified into two broad categories. One point of view stated that thought is a product of human consciousness when interacting with the inner and outer world. In this sense, thought is dependent upon people's physical and psychic faculties (see Table 1). The other viewpoint finds thought to be the es-

---

Thought Is:

"Man's attempt to comprehend his realization of the universe and to cope with what he can and cannot comprehend."

"An everliving, self-renewing process of imagination."

"The interpretation of intuition. Thought orders our experiences into conceptual knowledge to be used and transformed into constructive action."

"Mental pictures based on abstractions of our sensory modality."

"The visualization of objective, subjective, and subconscious possibilities."

"Reality. Everything we perceive is in terms of thought."

"The sum tool of all the mental processes by which ideas are formed."

"Thought generates speech. Speech in turn generates thought."

Table 1

Thought Is:

"The essence of Being. This thought causes all things in the universe to develop and evolve."

"The third point of the triangle which results from a combination of Spirit Energy and Vital Life Force."

"Reflection. It is the universe looking at itself."

"The infinite expression of the One Mind commonly called God—the Cosmos, Universal Soul."

"The expression of the creative faculty of the Universal Mind (God) which is also reflected in man."

"Thought in its most pure state is a constant vibration, emanating from the supreme energy and creative mind of God."

"The universe is a thought in the mind of God."

Table 2

sence of all that exists. According to this idea, thought is the creative force or principle of the universe (See Table 2). Proponents for both viewpoints describe thought as a tool which people use to understand themselves and their place in the universe. In this sense thought is seen as a process for transformation.

We use thought to acquire new information about our inner and outer worlds and to analyze the beliefs we hold. When we compare new observations and ideas with our current belief systems, questions arise. These questions are refined through further observation, analysis, and communication of ideas with other people. After we "let go" of our grip on the question, *intuition* silently unifies our diverse ideas and shows us a new and different way of looking through our images. Through the process of thought, our

Fig. 6. *"Thought is like unto a large running river, sometimes running deep, filling peoples' minds, sometimes running almost aimlessly. At one point of the river are somewhat materialistic thoughts—at another point are divine thoughts; duality."*

Note: *This figure and the accompanying caption, as well as those of the following three figures, were submitted by participants in the "Rosicrucians Thinking Together" experiment.*

beliefs are continuously transformed into more encompassing and useful realities. The more we learn through thought, the larger our frontier of knowledge becomes, and the more questions we have about the unknown. As one member stated: "Thought is an everliving, self-renewing process of imagination."

Images, then, are processed on three different levels. On the physical level we realize our objective sensations in terms of images stemming from sight, sound, odor, touch, and taste. On the mental (or ideation) level, images are processed by our faculties of inductive and deductive reason to form judgments and opinions. On the symbolic or soul level images are stored as memory patterns which can be recollected and recombined by the intuition to produce different forms of imaginative ideas or images. At this symbolic or soul level our thoughts acquire meaning, significance, and purpose.

Two elements that go into the thought process are desire and will, which provide the impulse for all thinking and activity; observation and the senses which provide the raw material and experience for complete memory; the emotional content that kindles and colors it; reason and analysis which gives to thought a form and an order; the imagination and visualization that allows thought to assume meaningful shape; and the faith based on knowledge that sustains it (see the quotation for Figure 7).

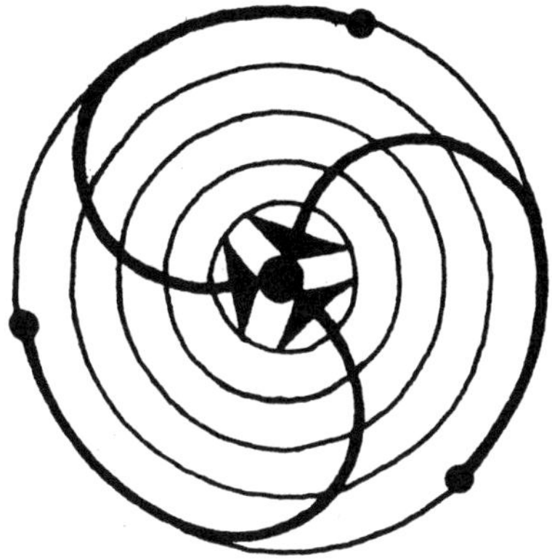

Fig. 7. *"Thinking is an act of the soul whereby it becomes conscious of itself and of other things outside itself."*

Thought is the innermost expression of the human consciousness, the whisperings of the self, the mind in action, directed awareness. It is accompanied by certain molecular movements in the brain and nervous system that produce ionic, electric, and magnetic vibrations. At the same time there is a tendency in thought to seek expression in the subconscious movement toward physical creation and manifestation which is patterned after the forms of inner symbolic realities. A thought does not necessarily consist of labels or words, but rather a psychic glow, which may or may not be expressed in words (see quotation for Figure 8).

Fig. 8. *"As the particles of light radiate in all directions from the Sun, and upon striking a prism, are diffused into rays of various colors, so perpetual thought emanates from the Universal Mind, strikes the prismatic mind of man, and becomes diffused into a variety of meaning, each mind imprinting upon it its own particular vibration."*

THE IMAGES IN MAN

At the beginning of this chapter we saw that thought-images are the building blocks of imagination, reason, and perception. We saw that thoughts are useful because their movement in the mind corresponds with changes taking place in the external world. In the next two parts of this chapter we will examine the way many Mindquest contributors interpreted the relationship of thoughts to themselves and the universe. An attempt will be made to integrate the two different views: that we are thought, versus that the universe is thought. Most participants in the Masterthought Experiment expressed the idea that thought was either a product of human consciousness or that thought was the essence of the universe. To explore these two points of view further, we will ask ourselves the question, "How does thought relate to ourselves?"

According to participants in the Mindquest program, our thoughts determine the kind of "psychic atmosphere" that surrounds us. Thus, to these participants it is essential that our thoughts be salutary and wholesome in character, as otherwise they can prove injurious to the mind and body. Positive and courageous thoughts create a healthy "atmosphere" and attract beneficent responses and influences from others. By allowing the mind to dwell on depressing and/or anxious thoughts we often create the very conditions we want to avoid. In the Bible, Job cursing his fate exclaims, "The thing I greatly feared is come upon me, and that which I was afraid of is come unto me." —Job 3:25.

The implications are that productive thought united with rectitude of spirit results in wisdom. Our attitudes and actions are often the direct result of our thoughts. By affect-

Fig. 9. "... *In certain senses God, the Cosmos, and Man can be regarded as within each other, but they still remain distinctive ideas, and in no real sense equal. Nor must it be forgotten that all things, of which the human mind can hold any conception, are for ever within the One Inconceivable Godhead, Who is of necessity before all and beyond all.*"

—*The Divine Pymander*

ing the autonomic nervous system, our thoughts and attitudes may manifest in the body as radiant health or psychosomatic disease. Thoughts are, therefore, intimately associated with our physical body.

One further implication of a contemplation of thought is that our conscious thoughts arise from the subconscious. Once thoughts become conscious we can discriminate among them. We can choose to flow with certain thoughts and let others pass by. The thoughts in our conscious mind again sink into the subconscious and there become seeds for new thoughts. Hence, this cycling of thought is an ever renewing source for creativity and inspiration, leading the imager to experiences of an expanding consciousness.

To these participants, thought was felt to generate a series of radiating and vibratory impulses that have psychic and ultimately physical properties, so that any thought sustained in the mind over a period of time intensifies and accumulates energy. Psychoanalysts speak of a *cathexis* (Greek for "holding"), the accumulation of psychic energy which infuses a particular idea. Cathexis is said to be high when a person strongly feels, concentrates hard, and vividly imagines. It builds up like an electric battery which constantly seeks to discharge itself, or, in other words, to find expression and fulfillment. In the case of hatred, the cathected energy seeks an outlet in aggression; in a humorous situation, in laughter; in a loving relationship, in kindness, benevolence, and knowledge. As one contributor said, "When archetypal energies become vividly experienced in the imagination, they must necessarily manifest in our outer reality."

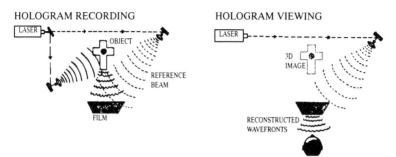

Fig. 10. *To record a hologram, laser light is split in two and bounced off mirrors through microscope lenses. Most of the light from the first beam illuminates the object, which reflects a complex wave pattern onto the film. The second beam serves as a reference wave, overlapping and interfering with the object wave (just like the meeting of two waves resulting from two rocks being thrown into a pool of water). The meeting of the two beams creates an interference pattern on the film that appears as a pattern of swirls. The exposed, processed film is a hologram, visible in any laser light that duplicates the original reference wave. The swirls in the hologram diffract this light, exactly duplicating the object wave. This wave is projected toward the observer who sees a three-dimensional image as through a window. Even a part of the hologram is capable of reconstructing the entire three-dimensional image, although the intensity and the perspective will correspond to the portion of the hologram used. See text for how modern neuroscientists have discovered analogous mechanisms in their study of thought and the operations of the mind.*

In creating a reality, the energies and structure of the mind may operate like a hologram. A hologram is a light interference pattern stored on an ordinary photographic plate which can be reassembled and projected as a three-dimensional image in space. To make the interference pattern and to project the three-dimensional image, coherent light from a laser is used. As shown in Figure 10 when coherent light from the laser is focused on an object bounced off mirrors and onto an ordinary photographic plate, a hologram negative is made. This does not take the form of a negative image as in ordinary photography. Instead, the "negative" is one of a wave pattern of swirls. When coherent laser light is transmitted through the hologram, a three-dimensional image is projected. If the hologram is cut in half or in quarters, the entire image is still projected from each piece, but it is only one-half or one-quarter as intense. Furthermore, each piece of the negative shows the three-dimensional image from a different point of view or perspective.

The studies and theories of several modern schools of neuroscience suggest that our brains may form thought-images in a way that is analogous to holography.[1] For thirty years, the brain scientist Karl Lashley searched for an *engram,* that is, the substance and site of a memory image. He trained experimental animals, then selectively removed portions of their brains (cerebral cortex), sometimes fifty percent or more, hoping to scoop out the exact part that contained the memory. His search never succeeded. Instead, Lashley was continually frustrated by the same finding: no matter what part was removed, it proved impossible to eradicate what had been taught. As if it were a hologram, the only correlation was that the intensity of memory loss depended on the amount of cortex removed, regardless of from where it was removed.

Corresponding to the hologram model of brain function is the *neuron ensemble* or *statistical configuration theory.* The ensemble configuration theories explain how the same group of neurons respond to various stimuli, but with different response patterns and, also, how a single neuron can participate in more than one thought-image. According to these theories a thought or a memory engram functions somewhat like the grid of lights that spells out a movie title on a marquee, or the headlines atop the Allied Chemical Tower in New York City (see Figure 11).

When the brain is at rest, isolated neuronal cells spontaneously fire in random patterns which sweep through entire populations of neuronal cells to form a unique configuration in the brain. As animals continue to perform their tasks, these established brainwave patterns grow stronger. Thus, wherever a specific thought is recollected, a unique wave pattern signifying the thought is released throughout numerous regions of the brain. This wave pattern, or field, is stable and can be recalled even when parts of the brain are severely damaged, such as Lashley's studies indicated.

The ensemble-configuration theory accounts for the fact that learning causes synchronization of a large number of neurons; this involves excitation of certain nerve cells and inhibition of others. Data suggest that each new experience creates a physical representation with a specific energy-field geometry in the brain. But exactly what shape this geometry takes and how it is consolidated into a thought is not explained by the ensemble-configuration theory. The hologram model would suggest that the energy field geometry is similar to the hologram's swirling interference pattern of light energy. The focus of attention would produce a multidimensional thought-image, including sight, sound, smell, taste, and touch components, in the same manner as a three-dimensional image is projected from the hologram.

It may be that not only the mind but the entire universe operates like a hologram.[2] The theories and publications of

BRAIN AT REST

Fig. 11. The Hologramic Thought Image. *According to one "electrical" theory, thought may function somewhat like the grid of lights that spell out headlines atop the Allied Chemical Tower in Times Square. When the brain is at rest, isolated nerve calls spontaneously fire in random patterns; messages are conveyed when certain bulbs light up and others remain "blank." Recalling the thought-image of the Rose-Croix consists of sequences of electrical patterns sweeping through entire populations of nerve cells to form a unique configuration in the brain. In actual fact, the brain does not construct thought images as if it were projecting images onto a movie screen. The neuronal configuration of an "image" may look more like the pattern in the top diagram. See text for details on how such a pattern could be interpreted as a thought-image.*

RECOLLECTION OF IMAGE

physicist David Bohm describe the nature of the universe as an enfolded order something like a hologram. The *enfolded order* consists of a realm of frequencies and potentialities underlying an illusion of concreteness. The concrete, unfolded aspect of things is a secondary manifestation. These appearances are abstracted from the intangible, invisible flux that is not comprised of parts, but of an inseparable interconnectedness. From the vantage point of this reality model, the universe itself begins to look very much like a Thought—a reality suggested by many mystics and Rosicrucians of old, and by a number of Masterthought contributors. Neuroscientist Karl Pribram and physicist Itzhak Bentov add that the brain may be a hologram interpreting a holographic universe. In mystical terms, "man's thought interprets and experiences universal Thought."

This model of the universe offers an explanation for experiences of illumination, transcendence, ESP, and altered states of consciousness where there is an access to the energy and force field domain—the primary actuality. According to this view, thought-images are a part of each other, interconnected by a universal hologram. Could this hologram be the direct result of the dual energy/force that Rosicrucians call Nous?

In this view, thoughts are affected by, and themselves effect, other thoughts. Inner experiences of timeless space and unity may correspond to a neural attunement with the primary actuality, the primordial hologram, the universal Thought. Inner experiences of connectedness, of time and of space may correspond to the substantial images of the universe. These images point to the separate parts of the outer world and suggest that everything is related.

Thought, then, enables us to see the reality of relationships and to assume the actuality of experience. It carves the world into tiny pieces. The more relationships one can perceive among these pieces, the more we come to realize how everything in the universe is related to everything else. Through thought we come to appreciate both the unity and the diversity of all that exists. Since thought constitutes our inner and outer realities, then shared realities can bind us together, allowing us to live in harmony with each other. The more universal the thought we share, the more universal is the community in which we live. Minds attuned with other minds work *synergistically*; that is, the expressed energy of minds thinking together is greater than the sum of energy separately expressed by minds that are not in accord. In holographic terms, the intensity is greater because more of the total mind is being used to project the reality image.

Similarly, thought is the basis of language which permits the sharing of the variously perceived facets of truth. Expressed thought binds people together in shared beliefs and opinions, or challenges them to clarify and identify their own ideas if opposed. Thinking becomes synergistic when individuals direct their thoughts to the same subject or idea. What is known as *group-thought* involves the combined mental energy of several people directed to a specific objective. It is in these ways that Rosicrucians Thinking Together work to bring forth in the world the greater light of understanding. As a light in a darkened room, these Rosicrucians strive to bring to humanity their own love of knowledge and their knowledge of a universal love.

Thought, then, becomes the *innermost expression* of human consciousness. Thought gives form to experience. Thought enables people to be aware of what they do, what they have done, and enables them to plan ahead. Our own individual thought creates our reality. Universal Thought creates actuality. Without thought, man would not exist to himself. As one contributor explained, "Our consciousness of thought superimposes on the existence of our inner and outer world the fact that thoughts are known. The world becomes a demonstrable world as man confirms its existence for the Creator."

What the hologram model does not explain is: Who does the looking? What is it that perceives the thought-image created out of the swirling energy patterns that make up the substance and force of thought? We can seek the perceiver as we explore the third question, "Does thought have meaning and purpose?"

THE HIDDEN MEANING WITHIN THOUGHT

As discussed previously in this chapter, thoughts are the images from which realities are created. Thought-images are the ever-living, self-renewing building blocks in imagination, in reason, and in perception. Thought is useful because the movement of images in the mind can correspond with changes taking place in the external world. The reason that a correspondence exists between mind and universe may be that both operate in analogous ways. From the vantage of a hologramic model, the universe looks much like a thought.

A. CREATION

"Thought is necessary to the manifestation of the universe."

"Thoughts require action to have purpose."

"Thoughts are needed to bring creative forces into usable form."

"The universe is sustained and ordered by thought. On the personal level, thought can be said to be the crucible in which human desires are transmuted into realities."

B. EVOLUTION

"The purpose of thought is to change man from a passive-responding animal into an active participant of creation."

"The purpose of thought is to advance life forms."

"The purpose of thought is survival. Living things will die without an ongoing fulfillment of purpose and thought."

"Man may be an approach to an ultimate thought form."

1. Transcendence:

"Elevation to higher planes of awareness."

"Elevation to a state beyond thought—to a state of absolute unity, beauty, light, harmony."

2. Self-Realization:

"Realizations of unity, essence, and meaning."

"Self-realization in order to achieve goals."

3. Culture Formation:

"The purpose behind the elementary ideas or germinal ideas from which the social structure has been developed."

"Thought is the primary image leading to the manifestation of certain patterns of associated ideas that may be recognized in all types of culture."

4. Communication:

"Communication allows new opportunity to live virtuous lives in harmony and at peace with other men."

"Communication teaches man to assume self-responsibility."

C. UNIFICATION, SYNTHESIS, AND MEANING:

1. Unity:

"The power of thought is increased as thoughts are combined."
"A single thought in harmony with 'universal' thought will be strengthened."
"The sum of thought is greater than the separate thoughts making it up."
"To bridge the gap between material energy and force."
"To think together—to realize the brotherhood of man."
"To bring order out of chaos."
"To bring oneness with God."
"To bring about a marriage of mind."

2. Knowledge and Insight:

"To achieve goals."
"To explore possibilities."
"To assign probabilities."
"To provide light on man's path."
"To discover natural law and invention."
"To gain understanding of what brings about thought."
"To allow man's reflected view to mirror the image of the creative force."
"To reach a satisfactory conclusion to any situation."
"To create realities."

3. Meaning and Significance:

"The universal purpose of thought lies in its very essentiality; in its essence lies the means for its expression, execution, and fulfillment."
"Thought illumines the meaning, purpose, and significance in man's universe. This is because thought gives visible form to the invisible."
"Thought is a formative, elemental symbol. Its purpose is to be."
"Divine Mind does not have purpose. It is purpose."

Table 3. (both pages) *THE PURPOSE OF THOUGHT IS: to allow for the creative evolution of Being, the creative evolution as a process of BECOMING. Thought is universal imagery in an ongoing process of becoming. The many ideas which contributed to the formulation of this "purpose" are summarized and outlined above.*

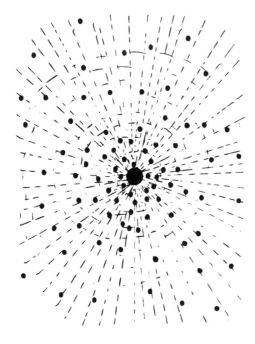

Fig. 12.
One contributor's sym-
bol for thought. The
small circles represent
data being drawn to-
ward the center and as-
similated by the mind in
increasing degrees of
understanding.

Some participants feel that thought does not have a purpose. According to this view, purpose is a philosophical concept invented by human thought. Therefore, the idea of purpose can only be expressed in relationship to human participation and intelligence. Several participants suggested that "thought creates purpose, but thought itself has no purpose."

The majority of participants felt that a purpose could be ascribed to thought. As summarized and tabulated in Table 3, the purpose of thought may be that of creative evolution, transcendence, self-realization, culture formation, meaningful knowledge, insight, and reintegration. These ideas might be summarized by the statement, *the purpose of thought is the creative evolution of Being.* For humans the statement might read, *the purpose of thought is the creative evolution of humanity's realization of Being.*

According to the Rosicrucian ontological model, the two basic components of being are energy (Spirit Energy) and force (Vital Life Force). Force is the organizing principle or intelligence of being; and energy is the "substance" that is organized (see Figure 13). The structure of both thought and the universe are related in that both consist of this energy and force. The force of being organizes energy into subatomic particles, atoms, molecules, living organisms, planets and stars. In the human mind, the force of being organizes energy into archetypes, images, ideas, symbols, realities, and initiatory experiences.

Even the behavior of universe and mind is similar. In the universe energy patterns are continually transformed. Stars and planets are continuously created and destroyed in the metamorphosis of matter. Thoughts, too, melt and coalesce in continuous cycles of transformation and rebirth as old realizations grow and transform into new and more useful realities. In the universe, matter and energy are interchangeable under appropriate conditions. In the mind, thought-images and energy are also interchangeable. This may be experienced in moments of insight, illumination, or altered consciousness.

One of the most serious challenges facing the neophyte is to move toward an intelligent open-mindedness. This does not mean that we must reject or abandon the experience or knowledge we have already gained. What it does mean is that, as creative imagination permits us to do, we must tol-

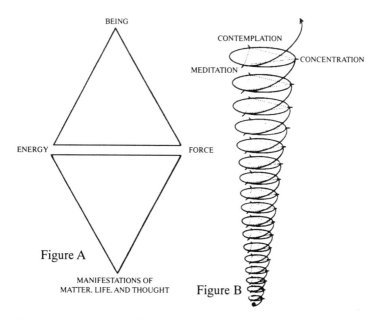

Fig. 13 A: *A model of Mind and its manifestation.* Fig. B: *A model of spiraling planes of consciousness in which realities are continually transformed.*

erate ambiguities without anxiety, integrate concepts in our thinking that seem to be diametrically opposed on the surface, rely as much on our intuition as our intellectual analysis, validate, investigate and learn about new discoveries relevant to our inner goals and do so without fear. This is no easy task, for it requires us to commit ourselves to our purpose with the certainty that competence requires, while realizing that what we are now sure of may be proved "untrue" tomorrow and that every answer is but the parent to a host of new questions. The more we can understand and practice the art and science of creative thinking, the more we will be able to do just this.

Each neophyte, called by that still, quiet voice of conscience, eventually comes to the state of Being-at-One (of Being-in-Love) with what had previously seemed to be another outside himself. In such an assumption experience, there is a realization of the greater Self. Being then becomes realized as indivisible. As we forsake the thoughts of separate being, we become more universal. We witness the universe imaged within our Self.

Three important questions—*What is thought?, What is the Universe?,* and *How are the two related?*—are resolved in the realization that man is mind and contains images of a universe as a reflection of himself, Being. Separate desires for knowledge, happiness, and immortality can then be "imaged" as a single force—to be. The Self then realizes what it is to be Self-conscious. With Self-consciousness, Being can become the perceiver of Being. The initiate then drinks from his own sacred stream and therein quenches his thirst for higher evolution. He is fulfilled. He is returned to his beginning. As expressed by T. S. Eliot,

> We shall not cease from exploration
> And the end of all exploring
> Will be to arrive where we started
> And know the place for the first time.

As symbolized in Figure 13, our thoughts move through spiraling planes of consciousness in which our realities of Being are continually transformed. Each turn of the spiral returns us to a beginning which holds a greater potential for unfoldment.

Having realized that a "thought" is not an independent entity, but an imaged representation of subconscious energies and forces, and having also realized that a "person," is likewise not an independent entity, but a symbolic representation of cosmic energies and forces, there are no thoughts, no entities which are constant and self-contained. A person is a being through which universal forces work. A thought is an imaged idea through which human forces work. These forces are both constructive and destructive. Both are essential in the universal cycles of energy exchange, the formation and disintegration of ideas and forms.

The concept of duality arises, for example, when it is believed that there is a "me" writing and "another" reading, or when it is believed that there is a "me" speaking and "another" listening. In our reality we perceive separate images that give rise to differences in experience and meaning. Perception involves both physically distinct sensations and our interpretations and re-creation of them in our mind, so that the elements are often rearranged into new form. It also involves understanding the mutability or changeableness of these, their transformation into each other, their transmutability in the alchemical sense. In other words, the essence—the totality—of "perception," which produces the key to wholeness and self-mastery, is its impermanence and illusory characteristics on the physical plane and its timeless, spaceless infinity on higher levels.

The human is formed as a vehicle for Being, but it is through words as appearances of learning and separation that he falls into ignorance. Through words and images as an expression of knowledge (directly felt experience) the initiate is raised again and again so that the One Self, the One Being, realizes more of its actual Self. Thought which recollects knowledge of the actual is not merely learned. As a seed it is already there within. One purpose of Rosicrucian philosophy is to provide an atmosphere where the initiate may harmoniously participate in the unfolding experience of the flowering of Being.

Fig. 14 A: *"I imagine the rain-bow in color as a universal of thought for the following reasons: 1. It appears to be a connecting line or bridge from one point to another. 2. It has no beginning and no end. 3. It is intangible and elusive. 4. It can be weak or strong, clear or hazy. 5. It makes something where there was noth-ing. 6. It is colored by atmo-spheric conditions as thought is colored by emotion. 7. To go be-yond the rainbow to the prover-bial 'pot of gold' has been man's dream. To go beyond thought is to transcend into light and perfect beauty, to achieve Cosmic Con-sciousnsness."*

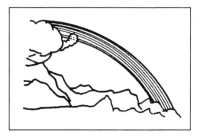

Fig. 14 B: *"Thought is the vehicle by which the universal conscious-ness progresses to the higher spiritual state."*

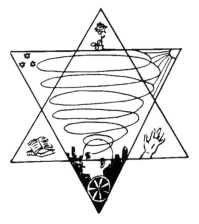

Fig. 14. *Symbols and accompanying quotations were submitted by par-ticipants in the "Rosicrucians Thinking Together" experiment.*

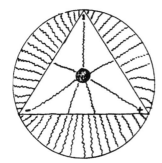

Fig. 14 C: *"Being does not state a purpose; it just is. The existence of natural laws indicates that repetition of cycles, disappearance of one form and emergence of another—anything necessary will be done to ensure the ongoing of Being. And it is going to fill the circle of all that is. Differentiation, the focalization of Being into personality, results in purpose. The personal mind, because of limitation, sees direction and value in thought and therefore assigns it a purpose. Therefore, purpose would be the reality for individuals and groups. If there is universal purpose in actuality, we can never get closer to it than reality. But were we created to give purpose to Being?"*

Fig. 14 D: *"Thought is awareness. It is Being. It is a state of experiencing the now. Thought gives man a conscious realization of himself and his surroundings. If this were not so, He would not exist to himself."*

CHAPTER 4

SYMBOL INTERPRETATION

CONFIDENCE: THE UNFOLDING SEED

In the supreme initiation of the Eleusinian Mysteries there was displayed for the initiate or *mystes* an ear of grain, grown and silently harvested out of season. The seed was, for the *mystes*, a miracle that captured the sense of wonder and confidence that can follow a sudden inner experience of the miraculous gift that life is for humanity.

Ancient man came to expect life to wax and wane according to the seasons of the year. Persephone would spend part of the year in the underworld and part of the year in flower and fruition. Year after year of regular cyclic experience led many people to believe that they should receive life's gifts at particular times. Yet, gifts can cease to be gifts when we expect them. They lose their capacity to surprise and delight, to shock and awaken us to new ways of thinking, to spontaneously arouse our heightened consciousness. Life becomes ordinary, drab, uninspiring when we know what we deserve and what we ought to have right now. We count on life to be predictable, to behave in a regular way, and if it does not, we become upset and lose our confidence in life.

And do we have complaints! "We've gotten too much rain this year and now we have floods!" Or, "We've gotten too little rain this year and now we have a drought!" "Can't count on the weather—can't trust it!"

"Education is a mess. You can't trust the teachers to teach Junior to read!" Others ask, "How can we trust politicians? Who elected them, anyway?" And who hasn't heard, "How can anyone be confident in banks—just look at these interest rates!"

Many people today have lost confidence in life. Life does not meet our expectations of what we think it should be. If people today have lost such confidence, this is a reflection of a greater loss of confidence in the divinity within ourselves.

When we lose our job, when we cannot afford a house we think we should have and deserve to have, when we become seriously ill, when there appears to be little security and little hope for a better life in the future, we may have difficulty feeling confident. In a chaotic world, in a tumultuous world of strife, psychological studies appear to show that feelings of self-esteem and self-confidence follow experiences of success. If life is working out well (the way we want it to), then most people say that they feel confident. Sometimes this confidence promotes more success. Yet when life persistently becomes difficult and does not meet expectations, then suicide rates go up, and depression, cynicism, worry, and fear become the dominant emotional context of our lives.

The ancient world too was plagued by such cyclic loss of confidence. For this reason, a confidence solely based on outer-world success was not held by the ancient mystery schools to be sufficient for a person's true needs. Such confidence was known to be an ephemeral mask, cloaking a basic insecurity and a hunger for a genuine confidence that could be an unshakeable foundation throughout life.

Today many people still feel that if we could just learn more, read more books, and attend more lectures, we would finally succeed in overcoming the problems that life offers us. If we were just more successful, had more successful experiences, then we could be confident. Then we could rely on the ordered predictability of this world. However, the ancients observed that such a view often produced an illusion of self-esteem and confidence that rose to the heights of overweening pride or *hubris*, and sank to the depths of despair, depending on the temper of the times. Conversely, they observed that some people avoid some of the ups and downs as well as avoiding personal growth by developing an inflated self-confidence that might say, "If only people would listen to me, we would all be better off. I'm confident in my ability. It's other people who are messing up the world. It's other people you can't have confidence in."

Many self-help books would have us develop such a cloak of self-confidence. Rosicrucians often suggest that such a method does not work. As one Rosicrucian Imperator, Ralph M. Lewis, said, "To have merely a feeling of assumed confidence when we want to do anything is to fool ourselves and gain nothing."

The word *confidence*, made up of the Latin prefix *con-* "with" and *fidere* "to trust," means "with intense trust." Tracing the origins of this word we find associations with reliability, fidelity, commitment, help, support, consolation, truth. The word *confidence* is a powerful word. This is the foundation upon which people base their ability to fulfill their function in life and manifest their innermost desires. As another Rosicrucian Imperator, Dr. H. Spencer Lewis, put it, "The secret of success in all things having a mental or psychic foundation is genuine confidence, not blind faith or the cloak of mere belief. By genuine confidence we are led to the attainment of self-mastery."

People often think that confidence or trust is the result of learning. Actually, the practice of Rosicrucian exercises can demonstrate for us that it is our perceptions and realities that are the result of learning. In fact, perception is learning, reality is learning, for cause and effect are never separated. Rosicrucian students can attune with an inherent confidence because we come to know that the world is not governed by man-made laws. By practicing the Rosicrucian experiments and exercises we experience that the world is governed by a cosmic order or power. The power is in us but not of us. It is the power that keeps all things in a state of being, both orderly and creatively evolving. Through this power the initiate looks upon the world with confidence and intense trust. Once this universal or cosmic power has been consciously experienced and accepted, it becomes impossible—ridiculous—to trust the petty strengths and trivial successes of the mundane world. Who would attempt to fly with the wings of a sparrow when the mighty power of an eagle has been given? Who of us would place trust in the shabby offerings of outer successes and failures, when cosmic gifts are laid before us?

In our previous exercise (found in Chapter 2) we were able to reach insight through what could be called *inductive thinking*. In the exercise we moved from objective reality (concentration on a specific object) to a symbolic reality (realization of a general principle). However, it is also possible to experience meaningful insights by reversing this process. We can proceed from a symbolic reality to an objective reality. This *deductive* approach is an aid to us in understanding works of art, dreams, and symbols received in meditation. The deductive approach is also of assistance in understanding the nature and qualities of Self.

With this second approach we are again guided by asking ourselves a series of questions. These questions in their general form can be found in Appendix 2. Each question is designed to draw upon specific mental faculties. The first approach was demonstrated with the use of a candle flame. We shall demonstrate the second approach with an intangible quality of Self, that of confidence.

ON THE NATURE OF CONFIDENCE

The world today is beset with economic and social problems characterized by a lack of confidence, a lack of trust in ourselves, others, and our institutions. To the average person these problems may seem unsolvable and overwhelming. The mystic can come to know that events or forces that at one time seemed threatening can, through understanding, become our allies and become instruments for materializing the desires of our Inner Self. Let us join together in the Great Work of increasing that understanding to create greater harmony, peace, and unity in our lives, the lives of others, and our world.

You are invited to explore with us the nature of confidence, how it comes to us and influences our behavior. To do this, we will use a version of the Rosicrucian Thought Process specifically developed to relate confidence to life experience. With confidence we can realize our Mastery in Self.

The Rosicrucian Thought Process, consisting of Concentration, Contemplation and Meditation, is explained in the Rosicrucian monographs, and is discussed and amplified in Chapter 2 of this book. This process uses experiences and questions to explore various stages of objective and subjective consciousness. Using this process we can integrate our inner and outer worlds, resulting in a greater sense of wholeness and confidence.

We shall begin by experiencing something of the nature of confidence. As we do this, our first objective will be to pay attention to and observe bodily sensations or feelings. For instance, take a deep breath. How are you feeling right now? Notice your heartbeat, your breathing, and other body sensations. Are you feeling heavy or light, cold or warm, tight or expansive, diminished or confident, or are the feelings you are experiencing at this moment different? Whatever they are, breathe deeply and let those feelings expand and intensify. This is the base point, the beginning, for you. We will now approach confidence through three exercises. After doing each exercise, stop for a moment, consider what you experienced, then write a brief description of the feelings (bodily sensations) experienced.

Exercise A. Recall a moment of personal achievement, a moment of success, a moment in which you did things "right." How do you feel as you relive this experience? What does this experience do for your self-esteem, self-assurance, your confidence, your ability to trust yourself and others? If you were asked to try to do again what you did then, how would you feel? Would you be as successful now? As you experience this, keep noticing your feelings. Breathe deeply and allow these feelings to intensify. When you are ready, stop for a moment and then write a brief description of your feelings and experience.

Exercise B. Now recall an occasion when you failed in an important endeavor, that moment when you realized that you did something "wrong." How do you feel? What does this exercise do for your self-esteem, self-assurance, your sense of confidence, your ability to trust yourself and others? Would you be willing to repeat this experience again? Would you do things in the same way, or would you change your approach? Do you find it easier to recall successes or failures? What does this tell you about yourself? Now, how do you feel? Breathe deeply and allow your feelings to intensify. Continue noticing your feelings. When you are ready, stop for a moment and then write a brief description of your feelings and experience.

Exercise C. Now imagine what it might feel like if you were a seed—a seed just now opening, unfolding to the world, unfolding potentials that have lain dormant, asleep within you. You do not know how life will unfold from within you: as a root, a stem, a leaf, a bud, a blossom. How do you feel as you experience the surprises that occur as you unfold and are caught up in the adventure of living? What does this experience do for your self-esteem, self-assurance, your sense of confidence, your ability to trust yourself and others? Again, breathe deeply and allow your feelings to intensify. Be one with your feelings as you continue unfolding. When you are ready, stop for a moment, and then write a brief description of your feelings and experience.

Now expand your feelings to encompass the complete experience of confidence: Seed, Failure, Success. Compare your feelings as unfolding Seed, in Failure, in Success. How do you feel at this moment? What does this expanded sense of the feeling of all three experiences do for your self-esteem, self-assurance, your sense of confidence, your ability to trust yourself and others? Once again, breathe deeply, and allow your feelings to intensify. When you are ready, stop for a moment, then write a brief description of your overall experience and feelings.

Let us now explore these experiences by asking ourselves a few questions.

1. Summarize your experience in each of the three parts, Success, Failure, the Unfolding Seed. Which were the most exciting, the most pleasant, the least pleasant?

2. What did you learn about confidence from these three exercises? If what you learned could be represented as a picture, what would the picture look like? Draw it.

3. What is the underlying principle, the fundamental truth that you experienced about confidence? Express this truth in one or two words. How is this symbolized by your picture?

4. Does this principle work in yourself, in other people, in animals, in plants, in minerals, throughout nature?

5. Does this principle work differently in Success, in Failure, as the Unfolding Seed? Feel the process going on here. What is it? Describe how this principle, this fundamental truth works in the outer world.

6. Have your experiences changed your ideas about confidence in any way? If so, describe these changes.

7. What does confidence do for you? Complete the following statements: "With confidence I can . . . I do . . . I am . . . "

8. How in your everyday life can you use these insights gained during your experience with confidence?

9. Complete the following sentence: "Using my new understanding of confidence, I intend to be open to the following experiences during the next two weeks: . . ."

10. After two weeks complete the following statement: "As a result of my new level of understanding of confidence, the following has happened to me: . . ."

Readers of Mindquest were invited to participate in this experiment. Participants compared their recollections of past successes and failures to the visualized experience of being an unfolding seed whose growth and development flowed out of inherent forces which Rosicrucians refer to as *Vital Life Force* and the *Inner Self*. These participants obtained insight into their experiences by using the Thought Process of Concentration, Contemplation, Meditation.

Of the respondents, 56.5% discovered from their experience that confidence for them is based on an intense trust in the Vital Life Force represented by the seed, whereas13%

agree with the psychology books that state confidence is based on past successes. These results appear in Table 4.

One participant reported that she discovered "Confidence is . . . it exists . . . it's always there, actual. Success and failure are the realities." Another participant added, "Confidence is the acceptance of oneself with the Source and how we let it express."

Another participant clearly compared her experience to her expectations. "During the exercise I came to the realization that confidence came from within, deep within. I always thought that confidence is something we gain from experience. I saw myself as having confidence in one area, but not another. I always thought I would gain more confidence in weak areas as I had more and more experience in that area. As a result of the exercise I see that is the hard way . . . the long way." Another respondent continued this thought. "Confidence now has a capital 'C' in my realization. Once I allow the Inner Self to come through, confidence comes with it. I am confident I can achieve all the things I want to achieve by tuning in with the Inner Self.

Confidence based on Seed	56.5%
Confidence based on past success	13.0%
Unclear response	30.4%

Total respondents (46)

Table 4. *The Source of Confidence: Responses to the Experiment.*

The abilities are all there. I can now go into areas in which I lacked confidence and now have confidence."

That genuine confidence promotes growth by means of experiences of both success and failure was also indicated in these reports. For instance, one non-member wrote, "With confidence I can afford to make mistakes, to learn from my failures as well as my successes. I now see success and failure as two crutches propping me up. With confidence I will eventually outgrow my dependence on them."

As shown in Table 5, a majority (95.8%) found the recollection of failure unpleasant. Success was found to be pleasant by 53.3%. Pleasant and unpleasant, success and failure are judgmental dualities. Excitement, however, is more likely to be a feeling that spontaneously arises from within. Participants found the most exciting experience was that of the Vital Life Force (85.2%). As a participant in New Zealand put it, "Imagining my being an unfolding seed gives me a great delightful experience, always worth look-

Experience	Success (%)	Failure (%)	Seed (%)	Number participants responding to questions
Pleasant	53.3	0	46.7	30
Unpleasant	0	95.8	4.2	24
Exciting	7.4	7.4	85.2	27

Table 5. *Evaluations of Confidence Experiences*

ing forward to. Not knowing how life will unfold, and watching my potential reveal itself, is simply too wonderful to express in words, as it will all turn out even better than I can imagine (despite my personal reservations)."

The enthusiasm of a participant in Canada reflected the Rosicrucian position on genuine confidence. "This experience has given me the realization that confidence is not a facade or cover under which we shelter, but is a condition of life, even a privilege of life, always there to be realized."

The practical benefits a genuine confidence can afford was summed up by an English Rosicrucian student. "I always felt I lacked the confidence to interact with people . . . to express my feelings. Since participating in this exercise there have been some subtle changes to my approach to life. It has been easier to communicate with others, in particular, strangers. Also greater understanding for others and ways in which I can be of service to them is growing within my being."

ATTAINING CONFIDENCE

Genuine confidence, the foundation of self-mastery, is an attribute of our inner nature that is of particular significance to Rosicrucian students. For this reason, many students are willing to explore subjective feelings, beliefs, and experiences, so that they might discover within themselves the inner nature, operation, and practical significance of a genuine confidence.

In the second part of this chapter we explored our research participant's responses to an exploration of genuine confidence with use of the questions employed in the Rosi-crucian Thought Process. In agreement with many psychology texts, 13% of our research participants experienced confidence as an attitude based on past experiences of success. For another 57%, however, confidence was an attribute of being, something we experience when we are attuned with the Inner Self. It is an attribute of who we are when we are being ourselves.

If this is indeed what genuine confidence is, how do we come to experience this, rather than experiencing low self-esteem, unworthiness, and inadequacy? If confidence were merely based on past success, then all we would need is more and more success to be more and more confident. The methodology here seems simple: Always be right, good, and successful. Yet, does anyone experience life this way, as being always right, good, and successful? How much success do we need to experience before we are worthy of feeling confident? If we think that we are always right, are we not also heavy with pride, seemingly disconnected from life and other people? With a need to be right so as to feel confident, can we admit to ever being wrong? When we are wrong, do we not feel guilty, unworthy, depressed? How do we escape this trap? How can we experience the genuine confidence the ancient Rosicrucians so highly praised?

Answers to this question fell into five areas: letting go, attunement, flowing, wholeness, and love. For instance, one participant in the research project who expected to do poorly because he always felt that he lacked confidence, was amazed by the results of the exercise. While exploring a particularly painful area in which he usually failed, he came to a sudden insight about what was holding him back. "I was not aware that one's confidence was so directly linked to one's state of being, to one's attunement to the Cosmic and Inner Self. Such a direct relationship is truly amazing." Letting the Inner Self shine enabled this individual to realize his inner strength.

Another participant explained the process this way: "I learned that we all could have the confidence we want, but most of the time we block it and don't let it come through. Simply put, what it is, is. If one lets the Inner Self break through, from where all flows, he will be given inspiration, strength, and confidence. If the mechanism were a picture, it would be of a chain being broken by a sword, letting out the strength and confidence."

Another person described the flow of confidence that results when the protective walls come down. "As a sound wave goes through its cycles of positive and negative, it provides an individual tone. Eliminate either the positive or negative portion of the wave, and the wave ceases to be. The mechanism for experiencing confidence is always to

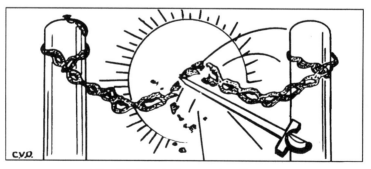

Fig. 15. *Truth Shatters the Chains.*

accept each moment of the day as a challenge to let the flow continue."

One individual had such a beautiful experience of the cosmic love connecting her to everything in the universe, that she was able to break through the many inhibitions that usually kept her from feeling confident. She writes, "Suddenly I am overwhelmed with love. It is within me at all times . . . I realize that Self is part of the Cosmic. I allow love, trust, and intuition to flood me with the realization that I am indeed confident."

One of the participants dealt with too much self-reliance. An inner realization of something greater than herself led to a personal insight. She states, "I realize that I had been excluding myself, withdrawing from the greater whole, and then trying to accomplish within myself things which needed the whole for expression. During the experience I had the sudden realization that the Sun does not shine in and for itself alone. It lights up our Earth and Moon, and all it meets as its rays speed on for all eternity. If its rays are an extension of or remain a part of the Sun, how greatly has the Sun expanded to embrace the Universe? We, too."

When people experience being who they are, they report feeling whole, attuned, connected; they experience unity, peace, love, joy, and gratitude; they feel confidence. One participant in the research project summed up the process as a series of steps. "Confidence is a gift I receive when I am who I am, when I let go and let the Inner Self direct. Thus, the first step is my willingness to be a walking question mark by letting go the blocks to an inner awareness of truth. That is, my letting go of the expectations and beliefs of what I think is true, even what I fear is true. Second, my mind now being silent, I can listen to my Inner Self and obey the inner promptings of my heart. Third, in this obedience I experience confidence, joy, contentment, freedom. Success and failure no longer matter; being true to Self does. Flowing through these steps I realize that living with my Inner Self is confidence."

Living with the excitement associated with confidence moved one of the participants to write, "Confidence is not the more or less static notion I used to conceive of, but is a dynamic, surprising, ever-adapting principle that can permeate my entire life. Why, this confidence is Self-mastery, isn't it?"

CONFIDENCE: THE MANIFESTATION

We all know what success feels like: the thrill, the excitement, the satisfaction. We know failure too: the pain, the despair, perhaps the shame. We desire success, the sense of power and control, the sense of safety we derive from consistently doing things right. The benefits from success are well known and well expounded in the world about us. Less known are the joys of a genuine confidence honored by the ancients and by modern Rosicrucians. Can the experience of a genuine confidence based on a trust in the Inner Self favorably compare with a confidence based on outer world successes?

Rosicrucians distinguish an *assumed confidence* advised as a requirement for success by many self-help books from the *genuine confidence* arising from a trust in the Inner Self.

The former relies on a seeming trust in outer, mundane conditions, while the latter confidence is a trust that requires no mundane reasons to support it. An assumed confidence requires external support, while a genuine confidence gives support. We wondered if the genuine confidence of the ancients could be readily experienced today in our modern world. Could the nature and the way of this kind of confidence be described in a manner understandable to the modern world? And could this confidence hold value for a productive person in modern society?

As a result of experiencing genuine confidence, participants discovered in their daily lives such mystical qualities of Self as wholeness, unity, love, peace, trust, contentment, creativity, enthusiasm, joy, freedom, and gratitude. For example, one member wrote, "I can be myself. I can let go and be free. I can experience more instead of expecting more. I feel like an oak tree dropping little acorns, watching these seed-ideas becoming new oak trees, and letting them grow on their own. I do not have to be concerned for them. Like the acorns these ideas can flourish on their own. Instead of my needing to be in control, now I am grateful to be able to watch and participate with confidence."

A member from Texas wrote that as a result of participating in the experiment, many unexpected things manifested in his life. "In my everyday life I can realize the continuity and unity that runs through all aspects of consciousness, with the constant realization that as I attune with the purity of the One, I am one and all is whole. I have cleansed my consciousness of many fears. It seems as if the dirty clothes I had been wearing during the past year have been laundered and cleaned with a lemon-fresh scent. Oftentimes, giving up old ideas and desires is hard, but confidence offers me the opportunity and ability to change with the effervescent flow of energy bubbling through all matter and all life forms in the Cosmic."

With a genuine confidence some participants report overcoming such problems as smoking, procrastination, lack of commitment, and the fear of forming new relationships. A respondent who had been having difficulty managing her life felt that, "With confidence I gain a clearer perspective. I am applying this new knowledge in my daily affairs, and feel I am now responsible again for my own life."

Another participant also reported trouble with managing time and with deciding what tasks to undertake first. This member found that decisions were made as she let her Inner Self through. "Picturing the list on my desk, I can pick one item at a time to accomplish. I can let my Inner Self do the picking and complete the task. I am finding that things are getting done one item at a time with no effort at all. The tasks are no longer overwhelming me at the start."

One member, choosing to deal with the problem of procrastination, used his new-found confidence to manifest the completion of several projects. "In the past two weeks this genuine confidence greatly aided my successful completion of several tasks in unfamiliar territories. Errors were next to non-existent and the results from my business ventures were gratifying, informative, and profitable. In my personal life I completed several social activities that had been put off due to insufficient confidence in the past. I was able to manifest all of this because I now see confidence works similarly in all situations. All 'different' situations in life are really part of the oneness of the universe."

Another member wrote expressing his gratitude for the opportunity to participate in the exercise because it had such a profound effect on his life. He wrote, "There have been subtle changes in my approach to life. I have noted, growing within my being, a greater understanding for others and ways in which I can be of service to them."

A participant also reports that genuine confidence allowed her to "solidify relationships," and "undertake a difficult master's degree program." Another member adds that with genuine confidence, "I can move through challenges with the inner support of knowing I am doing the right thing for me. With confidence I do whatever task is set before me. With confidence I am freed from emotional and selfish baggage and I am able to relate to others from a secure and loving place. I now see this truth is everyday life. It is the key to managing my daily affairs with love, and as I listen to the Inner Self, my daily affairs arrange themselves."

Another participant wrote that she always felt herself to be a victim. Due to a lack of confidence she felt that she was at the mercy of others and at the mercy of the environment. As a result of participating in the experiments she reports that she has begun "to eliminate self-doubt. I can now trust myself and others, for we are all instruments of the Cosmic. I am now more productive, for I truly believe I make a contribution to the environment."

"Since confidence comes from within," writes one member, "I can approach all areas with confidence." She found,

"Work and living circumstances are improving and I am now meeting financial obligations without worry."

Another participant reports, "Things I used to see as threats I now see as supports. I see them as feedback to support the overall picture. Confidence is assurance that the Cosmic gives us nothing that is not a support for us."

While genuine confidence is often accompanied by experiences of oneness, unity, love, wholeness, joy, peace, contentment, gratitude, humility, creativity, excitement, energy, and enthusiasm, the experience does not appeal to all. A few participants preferred to base their confidence on past outer-world successes. These participants also thought their confidence was beneficial and highly desirable.

A confidence based on outer-world successes " . . . gives me a better self-image and a more positive attitude." With success and confidence "I can walk, talk and argue with anyone, anywhere. I do things I know are right and beneficial to everyone. I am very sure of success in whatever I lay my hands on." With success, one member writes, "I can continue working alone, accomplishing what I can. I am still an idealistic failure to anyone who knows me, but it doesn't make quite as much difference anymore. Whether I get others' approval or not, as long as I know myself that I am not hurting others, not taking advantage, I can make myself happier without constantly feeling guilty for not having done more for everyone else first."

Confidence based on either outer-world success or on an intense trust in the Inner Self can apparently provide benefits. The results obtained here suggest that the former may support self-concepts of separateness, while the latter may promote self-concepts involving unity, oneness, and connectedness.

All the traits we aspire to as Rosicrucian students rest on confidence or intense trust. How often the student is told that once genuine self-confidence is achieved, all the other traits of self-mastery follow. Many mystical traditions and writings, including *Unto Thee I Grant*, point out that only the trusting can afford honesty, for only they can see its value. The trusting are inherently tolerant, for they have no need to judge others of the world. The trusting can afford to be gentle for harming others is the outcome of false judgment. Inner joy is an inevitable result of gentleness with others and with self. Thus, it also is a result of having tolerance and honesty and trust.

When we discover that we can be joyful living in this world of adventure and ever-new experience, we find we can be more open. We can become walking question marks, open-minded to what life has to teach us. Can we be open to the world and relationships if we are resistant, intolerant, dishonest with ourselves and others, untrusting? Without trust, can we be generous? Can we give away, release, and let go of our knowledge and accomplishments, sharing what we have with others that we may be open to receiving new gifts from life? Can we "let go" in the Rosicrucian sense, without trust?

Patience also is natural to those who trust, who have confidence. Those who are confident in the outcome, regardless of what it will be, can afford patience, to wait without anxiety, to anticipate events with joy and an open-hearted desire to learn, grow, and evolve.

To lead people to an experience of that cosmic power that creates in us confidence or intense trust, the ancient mystery schools gave worthy aspirants an opportunity for initiation. In reference to the Eleusinian Mysteries, Aristotle comments that the *mystes* or initiate was not meant to learn anything, but to suffer an experience and be moved. Perhaps this is what the Zen Master, Nan Sen, meant when he said, "Learning is not the path, intellect is not the Buddha." What then was the startling shock the *mystes* received when confronted by an ear of grain, grown out of season and silently harvested?

In prior ceremony and myth the *mystes* had become aware of the cycles of death and rebirth. The sacred ear of grain certainly gave the initiate the recollected certainty of life's continuity. A precious intellectual revelation, as we well know, but one that even many non-initiates were aware of. The ear of wheat in this context would not inspire in the initiate the confidence in his own fate that reports of the time would indicate, or the magic formula that was uttered would suggest: "And behold in this season when no grain grows, an ear of grain has grown." In fact, the ear of grain grown and maturing with supernatural suddenness is like the vine growing in a few hours in part of the revels of Dionysus; and we find the very same plant miracles in the nature festivals of many ancient cultures.

The ear of wheat suddenly grown, silently harvested and displayed to the *mystes* is really a mystical revelation—a revelation of the eternal cosmic principle within us, the principle that gave to humanity the fruit of life. This principle cannot be injured, cannot be destroyed, is actual and everlasting. Moreover, the revelation denotes an unexpected appearance of the eternal principle for a timeless moment in the mind and heart of the initiate.

Here we have the meaning of the display. This alone can account for the quiet beatific certainty conferred upon the initiate during the Supreme Eleusinian Initiation. Shocked by the ear of grain appearing out of time, and with the use of the ancient technique of assumption, the *mystes* becomes one with the grief of Demeter at the apparent loss of the daughter, Persephone, to the underworld of sleep, darkness and death; and one with the joy of Demeter at the return of her daughter in the spring of reawakened consciousness. In that timeless moment out of season, the *mystes* can plunge to the depths and rise to the heights of godlike feeling, yet remain at center still Self—timeless, actual, creative. In this moment the initiate gives birth to a confidence, an intense trust in the directive power of life and its power for renewal, adaptation, and evolution transcending ordinary human experience and expectation.

Upon deep reflection, perhaps, we too shall find that the meaning of such initiation and its experienced truth is all the more profound in that it does not make the initiate dependent on the favor of any single power or idea, but links the initiate through an experience of cosmic presence with the great movements and moments of a divine cosmos.

CHAPTER 5

BIRTH OF THE DIVINE CHILD

The Thought Processes (involving the principles and techniques of Concentration, Contemplation, Meditation, and Assumption) indicate that the human mind is a constellation of sensory information, feelings and emotions, inductive and deductive reasoning, modern and archaic memories, intuition and imagination. Thinking can use all of these faculties and qualities of the whole mind. The Rosicrucian Thought Process can assist in developing mental faculties, each in their proper place and time, so that each can contribute its part to the whole of our understanding.

Each stage of the Thought Process contributes to our experience of wholeness. Concentration exercises can increase awareness in the objective and subjective worlds. In contemplation our judgment and reason are used to discriminate and evaluate our sensory inputs and imaginative constructions. By discovering mechanisms of action and their practical application, we learn to master ourselves and balance our inner and outer worlds.

In meditation and assumption, confusion and disjointed thoughts can melt away, to be replaced by a unifying, healthful, and loving experience of the Inner Self. Imaginative impressions received in meditation and assumption give deeper meaning to the fruits of concentration and contemplation. They can explain the past, give insight into the present and indicate future possibilities. These psychic impressions and inner experiences can offer courses of action, guide us in decision making, and lead us to new insights to again be validated by observation, contemplation, and experience.

Insight, itself, is a result of a unification of all thought processes, including active and passive stages. Since creativity involves both doing and not-doing, we cannot force the process. However, through the application of principles like these, we come to understand the mechanism of creativity. We discover that we can use all of our conscious abilities to their fullest extent so as to meet life's challenges harmoniously. Then, we can relax the objective mind and release problems to the powers of the Inner Self. Below our conscious awareness, unconnected thoughts and observations shift and realign themselves, offering a solution or inspiration—often when we least expect it—one that we can contemplate further and possibly act upon.

Synchronicity is C.G. Jung's term for experiences which present us with meaningful coincidences in our lives. Synchronistic experiences associated with imagination, creativity, and mysticism are often difficult to communicate. Symbolic experiences often elude intellectual statements. If, for example, we were only to set forth a philosophy, we could proceed by setting forth the concepts involved. If we were interested in presenting a body of theoretical knowledge, we would proceed by presenting the assumptions, describing the evidence, and moving toward our conclusions in logical terms. We could analyze, delineate, and communicate our position by means of intellectual ideas. But in the mystical approach the primary material to be communicated is not only intellectual. The material to be communicated is a quality of our experience. The essence of this communication can be a tone or feeling. Tone and feeling are often what is lost in an intellectual statement.

In general, the poetic and mystical approach communicates concepts through the use of analogies and metaphors. Many years ago Alfred Adler made the remark that, "Man knows more than he understands." Adler calls to our attention that, while our knowledge of the world is worked out primarily by means of intellect, we also possess a way of knowing that operates by something other than rational procedures. If intellect and reason can be spoken of as operating on the "surface" of the mind, then this other aspect of knowing may lie much deeper. This knowing lies beneath the surface of conscious awareness. Describing our experience of what Adler spoke of as "greater than understanding," can be most difficult.

To speak of any experience of the psyche can be difficult. When we speak of the *levels* or *planes* of consciousness, we can understand that we are using an image and conception of *depth* and *height* only in a metaphoric sense. These terms are not meant literally. This metaphor of depth provided a fruitful context of thought ever since Freud began to think in terms of the strata of the unconscious. Freud, however, approached the depth of personality in terms of repression. This is the idea that a person living in society has certain urges and memories which he cannot bear and is unwilling either to express, experience, or remember; therefore, he represses them. Once they are repressed, Freud believed that they dropped into the unconscious. In the unconscious they were supposed to be transformed so that they were no longer expressed in literal form but were symbolized. Freud's model provided a basis for a pathology of the mind.

In contrast to this conception, Jung's model of the mind is similar to the mystical approach. Jung and the mystic study the subconscious in terms of a natural process of growth, transformation, and even transmutation of the psyche. The metaphor that is most appropriate is that of the seed or the unfolding rose. In the seed there is the potentiality that carries all the possibilities of what the full-grown species can become. Thus, the fullness of the oak tree is latent in the acorn. Similarly, between the depths and heights of man, the marriage of objective consciousness and the subconscious produces a new child of the mind—the bearer of human potentialities.

This symbolic child of the mind contains the possibilities for developments that are present in the individual, but which are not visible because they have not yet become manifest in life. We cannot see them until they begin, like the rose, to unfold and fulfill themselves in the outer world. For this the aspirant is willing to develop a capacity for observing the inward process of growth while it is still in motion. With this also come abilities to distinguish the corresponding opportunities for growth in the outer world of the senses. As we become more sensitive, attuning both inwardly and outwardly, we are able, with the balancing force of contemplative reason, to draw these potentialities forward. To provide an opportunity for this is a primary task of the Rosicrucian experience.

A *Child of the Mind* is a symbol of the future. The child is also symbolic of that stage of life when old forms of thinking are transformed and acquire a new simplicity. From this condition of transformation arises the conception of the mind's child as being symbolic of the Inner Self, the Mystic Center, the *Entheos* (God or divine force within). The Child of the Mind is of the Soul, a product of the conjunction of conscious and subconscious. In fact, one often dreams of a child when a great spiritual change is about to take place.

In Egyptian myth, Osiris (a Soul figure) is dismembered, taken apart and disassociated. He can be thought of as a symbol of the analytical mind and the left side of the brain. Isis (another Soul figure) reassembles Osiris, puts him back together and unites with him. She is a symbol of synthesis, imaginative thought, and the right side of the brain. The product of the marriage was Horus, the holy Child. Horus is a much revered symbol because he has the power to encompass all that Osiris and Isis separately represent. He was also a more ancient symbol than either Isis or Osiris. Horus or the Hawk was an emblem of the Soul and implied solar transfiguration. From Horus the figure of the phoenix was derived. The Phoenix is Horus before the throne of the Mystical Golden Dawn.

Jung has indicated that such powerful symbols appear as spontaneous images which emerge from the depth of the subconscious. They act as vehicles by which the potentiality latent in the subconscious is carried forward as "on wings of thought." The transforming symbol embodies the open future as that future is becoming the present in the open child-like recesses of the individual. The symbol provides the motive force by which this potentiality can unfold and become manifest in the world of form.

From this perspective, it seems most inadvisable to approach an imaginative symbol only in an analytical way. If we reduce our inner symbols to experiences of the past, we deprive them of their potentiality. Relying solely on analysis can result in a major error of interpretation because the symbol, as a factor of unfoldment, does not have its origins just in our past experience any more than the potentials of an egg are drawn just from the past experience of the chicken it is about to become. To break the symbol apart and analyze it before it has been completely experienced deprives the symbol of its power for life. Better to let the symbol live its life first before performing an autopsy and dissecting it. Thus, a more vital and productive way to work with symbols and thoughts is to work with them affirmatively, to encourage them, nurture them, and draw them forward by giving them life through the principles and techniques of assumption. By means of such life, the process of individual growth and unfoldment can proceed, moving through the symbol which functions as the active psychic vehicle for expansion of consciousness.

Many seekers come to the Rosicrucian Order feeling frustrated because their lives seem so meaningless to them. They may feel that if they could know the meaning of life, they could be more productive, fulfilled, and at peace within themselves. We wish to share our knowledge with them, but of course, we cannot do this in one easy lesson, or even in ten lessons for that matter! For we cannot tell a person what the meaning of life is. Each person comes to experience the meaning of life for himself and herself. Each person comes to be initiated into a meaningful life, for the experience of a meaningful life involves an intimate awareness.

A major part of the meaning of life is contained in the process of discovering it. Awareness of a meaningful life develops from an ongoing growth that is experienced through an ever-deepening contact with *actuality*, with *what is*. To speak as if this were an objective knowledge, like the War of 1812 between England and the United States, misses the point. The meaning of life is indeed objective when it is reached, but the way to it is by a path of subjectivities as well as objectivities. It is by way of a marriage of objective with the subjective, rational with irrational, analytical with imaginative. It requires a series of profound experiences within the privacy of the psychic self. The meaning of life cannot be told. It is a secret, a mystery. It *happens* to a person. A knowledge of the nature of thought and an awareness of one's own psyche is valuable in assisting this to happen, but meaning is a gift that is given to a person from within.

CHAPTER 6

THE SCIENCE OF INTUITION

Through the study of intuition the Rosicrucian reaches the frontier of intellectual and spiritual power. Rosicrucians learn that great progress in people's lives depends on the release and utilization of intuitive powers. No significant discovery, insight, or creative production has come about solely as a result of objective mental activity. Laboratory experiments as well as scores of interviews with scientists, writers, composers, and artists attest to the fact that solutions to problems are achieved only after they have been released to the subconscious or intuitive faculty of the mind.

Claude M. Bristol and Harold Sherman, in their book *T.N.T. or the Creative Power Within,* tell about Thomas Alva Edison's practice of taking multiple catnaps as he worked on an invention. When he felt blocked, after exerting himself to the utmost, Edison would lie down on his couch and fall asleep. He claims always to have received additional light on his problem.

The German psychiatrist Herbert Silberer experimented with this process by putting himself in a borderline state and trying to think through complicated problems he had been unable to solve in the normal waking state. He found that the complicated problem he was considering would disappear from awareness and would be replaced by a meaningful form of symbolic imagery. One problem Silberer contemplated was, "If intuition is universal, why do some people intuit to do one thing, while others intuit to do something else?" Silberer wrote:

> In a state of drowsiness I contemplate an abstract topic such as the nature of judgement valid for all people . . . . A struggle between active thinking and drowsiness sets in. The drowsiness becomes strong enough to disrupt normal thinking and to allow, in the twilight state so produced, the appearance of an auto-symbolic phenomenon. The content of my thought presents itself immediately in the form of a perceptual picture (for an instant apparently real): I see a big circle (or transparent sphere) in the air with people around it whose heads reach into the circle. This symbol expresses practically everything I was thinking of. The [universal] judgement is valid for all people without exception—the circle includes all the heads. The validity must have its grounds in commonality: the heads all belong in the same homogeneous sphere. Not all judgements are [universal]: the body and the limbs of the people are outside (below) the sphere as they stand on the ground as independent individuals. What had happened? In my drowsiness my abstract ideas were, without conscious interference, replaced by a perceptual picture, by a symbol. (See Figure 16)

Silberer goes on to say that he found this picture-thinking an easier form of thought than rational logic. Silberer

Fig. 16. *Silberer's symbolic conception of human judgments.*

conducted extensive experiments in the borderline state, considering complex, abstract thought and waiting attentively for symbolic images to appear. He found that his thoughts in this state always gave rise to images, thus demonstrating to him that the mind automatically transforms verbal information into unifying picture symbols. Another example Silberer gave is as follows: "My thought is: I am to improve a halting passage in an essay. Symbol: I see myself planing a piece of wood." He therefore proceeded to "shave" words from the essay.

In terms of the principles taught by the Rosicrucians, what Silberer did was to put himself in a receptive, borderline state; he introduced a problem he had already analyzed, and looked for an answer to appear as a receptive visualization. The results of his experiments demonstrated that problem-solving visualizations are often symbolic.

Imaginative images or symbols that spontaneously come to our awareness arise from beyond our objective consciousness. They come to us from an inner center, from an intuitive faculty of mind. They do so in their capacity to join inner and outer worlds, spiritual with material, invisible with visible, macrocosm with microcosm, imagination with objectivity, actuality with reality. If we are willing, they bring about for us a marriage of the mind.

Symbolic thinking can be an art of thinking in images rather than words. An image is expressed as a symbol to communicate a meaning beyond the obvious, beyond the grasp of reason. Because there are innumerable things beyond the range of objective, human understanding, we constantly use symbolic terms to represent concepts (such as infinity) that we cannot define or fully comprehend. The symbol, then, is a mechanism for understanding. It forms a bridge between a metaphysical world in which a Divine Mind encompasses All, and the physical world of the brain and senses in which All can never be perfectly known. In the physical world, no matter how powerful a telescope or microscope man builds, there always remains matter that cannot be seen even with the aided eye. The human physical senses, as complex and marvelous as they are, are limited in what they can perceive. Therefore, human knowledge gained through the physical senses can never be perfect or complete.

Contrary to popular belief, the scientific method combines *intuition* with objective observation to acquire new knowledge. New ideas come from intuition, without which the information we gather through random observation would be a meaningless train of facts. Intuition and reason bring the random observations together into a meaningful relationship and into an ordered system. *Experimentation* and *empirical observation* are methods for verifying and validating the new ideas already hypothesized by the intuition, thus adding these ideas into the realm of new knowledge.

In scientific research the key is to possess the insight that will enable one to ask the meaningful question. The answer is implicit in the question. The meaningful question is arrived at by transcending the older realities and the physical perceptions that are based on these older realities. The new symbol—the instrument of understanding—allows us to transcend the limits of old realities and perceptions. Goethe said, "In the symbol, the particular represents the general . . . as a living and momentary revelation of the inscrutable."

Intuitive symbols can reveal the essence of great truths that cannot be comprehended by the intellect alone. Symbols, by their nature, can resolve paradoxes and create order from disorder. In flashes of insight, they provide knowledge which joins dispersed, disparate fragments in a unitary vision. We see, if only for a moment, the greater scheme of things, the unity of the universe, and our place in it. We see unity in terms of form and image corresponding to the objective world surrounding us—the only things that are "seeable"—yet we now see these concrete images in a novel, non-ordinary light.

Intuitive cognition is apt to be unreliable unless preceded by (1) a willingness to have a transformed viewpoint, (2) a willingness to make an energetic effort to gain information, and (3) a willingness to conduct a scientific evaluation of the idea. The symbolic model or hypothesis can be evaluated by experience in the objective world. Thus, while symbolic models and intuitive hypotheses can be derived by proceeding stepwise through a process of concentration-contemplation-meditation, we return to an objective state of concentration so as to verify the validity of the intuited symbol.

If we allow it, our process of thought can be an ascending spiral, for in returning to concentration, more details are again observed; the return to contemplation reveals even more about the operation of the idea being considered; while a return to the borderline or meditative state may demonstrate that our intuited symbol can now explain more, and give meaning and significance to more aspects of the objective world than we previously realized. A return to the meditative state can also result in the transformation of the original realization into a more powerful symbol or model. The transformed symbol is now more powerful in the sense that it has the capacity to explain and predict more about nature (see Figures 17 and 18).

When the human mind approaches a basic problem such as the nature of matter, observations only provide raw data with which to begin. The observations themselves do not contain the concepts with which the data can be given significance and meaning. For example, a stone or a solid block of wood does not suggest the moving particles of matter in terms of which the atom is conceived. The conception of the atomic theory does not lie in the wood, but in the mind of the person who interprets what is seen. The image brought forth from the intuition proves

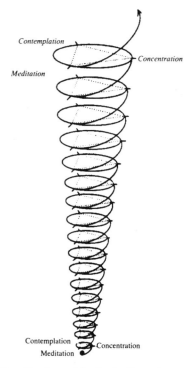

Fig. 17. *A model of spiraling planes of consciousness in which realities can be continually transformed by the repeated process of concentrative-contemplative-meditative experience.*

its value by its usefulness in interpreting raw data. Ultimately, the test of the image lies in facts of observation, as the image of the universe contained in Einstein's General Theory of Relativity required an eclipse to validate its insight.

Even when a symbolic image, as a theory, is verified in a specific case by external evidence, it still remains a working symbol whose "truth" is not absolute, but relative and metaphoric. A symbol is a reality and not an actuality. It is defined by the symbolic terms of the governing image, as the conception of the atom. This is the sense in which Einstein can say, "Physics is an attempt conceptually to grasp reality as it is thought independent of its being observed." The consequence of this approach followed by physics is a self-consistent version of reality marked off by the framework of the symbols it is using. At certain points this version of reality is tested by external observation, but its es-

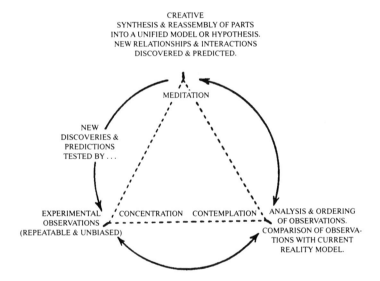

Fig. 18. *Correspondence of the methodologies of science and Rosicrucian mysticism. One of the basic tenets of both methodologies is the rejection of authority and dogma—the refusal to accept a statement just because someone says it is true. Rather, by keeping an open mind toward new realities and by using the process of concentration-contemplation-meditation, individuals come to self-knowledge and a knowledge of self.*

sence lies in the inner logic of its symbolic system. "In this sense," Einstein wrote, "we speak of physical reality."

Physical reality as Einstein defines the term, is not the commonsense reality of the physical world. It is not the stone we stub our toe on. Physical reality is rather the self-consistent body of knowledge implied by the symbol structure of modern physics. It is a reality defined by its framework of imagery. No claim is made that the image's portrait of "truth" is more than relative and partial; but it nonetheless greatly extends human knowledge and wisdom. By means of symbols the Rosicrucian student learns to direct the forces of nature.

Just as atomic physics opened access to a dimension of reality that had not been experienced before and made tremendous amounts of energy available to humans, so the growth and evolution of our personal realities and symbolic conceptions contact greater sources of personal strength and release greater powers of personality. To the Rosicrucian student, each and every shape, color, object, and action in the world is a visible form of a vibratory level of a primal thought existing beyond the sensate mind. These visible forms of vibration, like symbols, are capable of combination and rearrangement, giving rise to the innumerable nuances of knowledge. If we view the world of our senses in this way, we can become sensible to similar or corresponding moments within our experience. We can transcend the limitations of the physical world and enter the world of the Absolute. The genuine basis for intuitive symbolism, then, is the correspondence linking together orders of reality, binding them one to another, and consequently extending from the natural order as a whole to a Cosmic Order. By virtue of this correspondence, the whole of nature is but a symbol. Hence, the genuine significance of Nature becomes apparent as we allow it to be a pointer directing the willing heart to an experience of Cosmic Truth.

The parallel between physics and the Rosicrucian philosophy of mind is that both use symbolic concepts to set energy free; but there the parallel ends. The quality of their application is different. Each leads to a body of knowledge regarding its special segment of reality, but the Rosicrucian conception of mind and psychic reality leads to more than intellectual knowledge. It leads to disciplines for developing larger personal capacities for experience and fuller participation in dimensions of reality that reach beyond the individual.

CHAPTER 7

IMAGINATION

The exploration of the Marriage of the Mind was undertaken by many people, who brought their special expertise and experience to the investigation. During the twelve years of Mindquest and the AMORC Research Program, two people made a special contribution to the study of imagination, symbolic function, and dream, showing the relationship of these mental qualities to processes of thought and integration. In this chapter, the first section is written by June Schaa, who demonstrates the importance of our imagination to the integration of the whole person. In the second section, Michael Bukay indicates how a symbol can permeate our entire life experience. In the third section, we will explore mind-body integration, and in the fourth section, we will examine the contribution of our symbolic thinking to our health. From these discussions, we will gain the understanding that our imagination is a central feature of our life experience.

THE INWARD DREAM OF THE SOUL

Why is it that we cannot foresee clearly, definitely, and without limit into the future? Perhaps we limit imagination to the simple reproduction of what we already know. But true imagination is the inward dream of Soul; it is the poet's mirror in which the Cosmic is reflected. Rosicrucians have long taught that imagination is the divine gift of Soul. It is the principle which is behind aspiration, the basis for the four perfect states of being.[1] All aspiration is concerned with things that are conceived but not yet attained. Through this sublime idealism we can transform the world, converting it from what we conceive it to be. Imagination sheds illumination on the everyday world. With its wisdom Benjamin Franklin invented bifocal eyeglasses and Einstein discovered relativity.

Before attempting to understand the ways we may use imagination let us first distinguish it from other forms of the mental process. To begin with, imagination is often mistaken for *imaging,* a form of visualization that reproduces mental *images.*[2] Imagination includes imaging, but imaging and visualization need not be a form of imagination: they are, instead, related to "memory classification." As an illustration: Concentrate your awareness on a nearby object. If it is a tree, for example, notice its colors, textures, odors, sounds. Now close your eyes. Recollect in detail the object you observed. This is imaging. On the other hand, if we conceive a different use, an alteration or a transformation of our tree or favorite object, then we would be using imagination.

Imagination is also mistaken at times for the active inductive and deductive reasoning powers. Minute by minute we are going backward or forward, or both, in thought. Consciousness is never stationary when awake. Through the use of these subjective powers of reasoning we are enabled to ask questions, classify, and evaluate our perceptions. The more we reason or contemplate on either the sensory or imaginative information coming to us from without or within, the better we come to understand and utilize what we experience.

We have pointed out that imagination uses but is not the same thing as imaging, visualization, inductive, or deductive thinking. Imagination is not the product of concentration or contemplation, nor is it the passive state of awareness that leads to meditation. Instead, imagination reaches us through these three major channels of thought. If not these things, what then is imagination? Whence does it come?

According to Rosicrucian tradition, imagination is the supreme acting factor within the subconscious mind. It allows us to go beyond the limitation of space and time. Unlimited imagination uses a vast subconscious storehouse of memory which we refer to as *complete memory* or *Akashic Records.*[3] Creative imagination occurs when Akashic memory combines with intuition to bring together unrelated but known elements in a new and surprising manner.

Complete memory, intuition, and imagination form a supernal triangle on the immaterial plane. Ideal images appear upon the mirror of the meditative mind and are processed by reason, there to become the objects of the future. As illustration: In his imagination during 1865 Jules Verne took a well-detailed trip to the moon 100 years in advance of the actual moon landing. But futuristic ideas can also start with past events. Suppose I were to imagine how the earliest humans lived in prehistoric times. Here I am, then, imagining what seems to belong to the past. But if in my conception my imagined idea were to become a reality by means of scientific research, then my idea of the past would also be a present event, and any proof that would substantiate my imagined idea would make it a reality in the future. Schliemann uncovered Troy because he first imagined it to be a city that had physical existence.

How may we encourage the inspiration that comes from the use of higher imagination? There are several methods and a few simple exercises we will now explore. The first, *spontaneous imagination,* begins with an instant impression out of nowhere—one that suddenly "pops" into mind in connection to what we are doing at the moment. In order to stimulate spontaneous imagination, try the following exercise sometime today and frequently during the next week. Become especially aware of your surroundings. See yourself realizing what you perceive. This is good observation. As you see something while walking, be aware of what it is that you perceive. Discover the meaning it has for you. Total concentration on what we observe will open the door for subtle impressions to appear spontaneously. Suddenly we will become aware of a way to improve what we observe.

This profound exercise of becoming observant of the external world, while passively registering any intuitive impressions that may come, is not done necessarily to bring about changes in what we perceive. Rather, the exercise is intended to help us develop a healthy memory of everyday things, as well as building up an association of intuitive ideas. By continuous and concentrated observation, we will ultimately bring forth in the imagination, out of such experiences, a fruitful idea. Such ideas may be practical or inspiring; something that will in some way improve the lot of others while adding to the universal harmony.

You may recall that while observing an apple fall from a tree, Newton had an intuitive idea that led to the law of gravity. Newton combined spontaneous imagination with the second type of creative imagining called *determinative*. Determinative imagination is directly related to creative effort. It is used when we deliberately plan to bring about a change or transformation in something: i.e., when we set out to find a new source of energy.

Before activating determinative imagination we should be clear in our minds about *why* we desire to bring about a new idea or transformation in something. Defining motives and establishing goals may eliminate building a future problem instead of a boon for humanity. The next step involves conducting exhaustive researches into the subject in general, thus allowing spontaneous imagination to add changes to the existing object. When the necessary concentration and contemplation upon the desired subject has been fulfilled, the mind will naturally seek diversion. Now is the time to "let go" of our mental work and allow higher imagination to take over. And what better place to "let go" than in the midst of nature—the infinite source of cosmic correspondences! Newton sat, simply admiring nature, when an apple fell along with the answer to a temporarily forgotten question he had determined to solve.

Many of our great and cultural advances have come about through the use of spontaneous and determinative imagination. However, not everything we imagine is capable of becoming an inner and an outer reality. The vivifying power of imagination also lies behind fantasy, a word that has been widely misunderstood. In the past we have tended to equate fantasy with the unfulfilled, repressed or dream-like character of subjective memory which is no longer conscious. Instead, true fantasy, as mystics know it, has its roots in the higher Akashic memory of the subconscious. Today medical science is augmenting the traditional thought about fantasy. For example: the meaning and importance of fairy tales in the lives of children is being stressed by such noted psychiatrists as Bruno Bettelheim.[4] However, fantasy is not only a healthy form of imagination for children alone. It can also be used constructively by adults to bring about a desired transformation of personality. Psychologist J. M. Spiegelman adds new light to an old concept that when we direct our visualization from the psychological truth of imagination, we release a type of fantasy that reaches the universal, archetypal, and mythological level.[5]

New meanings and understanding come when we are not afraid to experiment with the images that the subconscious presents to us. Inspired ideas contain a secret connection which the seeker will always find hidden in nature or history.

Perhaps you have noticed that imagination—whether spontaneous, determinative, or mythological—requires the creative use of all faculties of mind working in harmony. This proper use of imagination is well illustrated by the medieval alchemists' pursuit of the Philosopher's Stone. They taught that the process of creation is performed outwardly through a chemical operation and inwardly through active imagination. "Old legends read in this new light reveal new possibilities; old dreams are rapidly passing into realities. The domain of the mystic is an unexplored dreamland, an endless wonderworld—the synthesis of the beautiful and the true: And the magical moon, whose golden orb illuminates it, is the 'shaping spirit of imagination.'"

THE CIRCLE: A GUIDE TO PERSONAL UNDERSTANDING

The circle is perhaps the most important mystical symbol ever used. Knowledge of the circle allowed the American Indians to penetrate beyond the veil of sensory illusion, map out the human consciousness, and gain a holistic understanding of their environment. The circle provided deep insight into the nature of Self and helped them to achieve unity of mind in a systematic way. The mysticism of the American Indian has much to offer the modern person. As a guide to personal understanding it is as universal today as it was hundreds of years ago.

The earliest mystical teachings given to Indian children concern perception and illusion. For instance, a teacher and a group of young Indians might go to the prairie and sit in a circle. Each child describes the play of light on an eagle feather placed in the center of the circle. The children observe that each individual sees a different image of the feather due to his or her unique position on the circle. They discover that there are as many ways to perceive the feather as there are points on a circle. The children also learn that individual perceptions are much more complicated than just position on the circle.

One Indian may be near-sighted, another far-sighted. Many are in-between. Some may be color-blind, and others completely blind. All perceive the feather differently due to individual differences in their senses.

On still another level, a psychological one, each Indian sees the feather in a unique way. One Indian may help make feathered headdresses for the chief, another may be allergic to feathers, and a third Indian may feel neutral toward feathers. Again, each child in the circle perceives a different image of the feather, this time due to past experiences with feathers.

Through this simple exercise with the circle, the Indians taught their children that there is an unlimited number of ways to perceive anything. All sense perception is illusory. What is important is not the actual nature of what is perceived, but the understanding of our perceptions and those of our brothers and sisters.

The circle, or *Medicine Wheel* as it is called, is the total universe and can be understood as the mirror in which our consciousness is reflected. "The universe is the mirror of the people," the old teachers say, "and each person is a mirror to every other person." Every idea, person, and thing can be seen as a mirror giving people the opportunity to discover Self—if we are willing to see our own reflection.

American Indian mysticism taught that each thing within the Universe Wheel, except man, knows of its harmony with every other thing. Only we are born with a fragmented view of the world. To achieve harmony we seek to understand our reflection in the Four Great Powers of the Medicine Wheel.

The Indians taught that at birth each person is given at least one of the Four Great Powers: wisdom, innocence, illumination, or introspection. The purpose of our spiritual

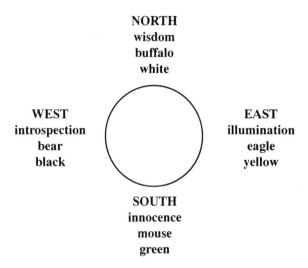

NORTH
wisdom
buffalo
white

WEST
introspection
bear
black

EAST
illumination
eagle
yellow

SOUTH
innocence
mouse
green

Fig. 19. *The American Indians taught that at birth each person is given one of the Four Great Powers of the Medicine Wheel: wisdom, innocence, illumination, or introspection. The purpose of man's spiritual existence is to obtain the remaining powers and become a whole person.*

existence is to obtain the remaining gifts and become a whole person.

The Indians symbolized each gift by a cardinal direction, an animal reflection, and a color (see Figure 19). For example, there are buffalo people, mice people, eagle people, and bear people. A buffalo person is born with the gift of intellect. A buffalo person's perception of the world is primarily a mental one. Like the north wind and snow, however, a buffalo person is cold. The intellect makes for a wise person, but one without feeling. A buffalo person must try to include the heart in decision making. This buffalo person must first seek the gift of the South.

A person born only with the gift of the South perceives the world like a mouse. Because of their habits, mice have an intimate touching and feeling relationship with the Earth, but cannot see beyond their immediate vision. Mice people cannot understand all they see and feel because they cannot connect their experiences with the rest of the world. A mouse person might first seek the gift of the East, the far-sighted vision of the eagle.

Eagle people can see clearly, far and wide, and into the future. Although very perceptive, they understand little of what they see. Eagle people are "above it all" and seldom touch the Earth. They are concerned primarily with outer experiences and have little knowledge of their inner world. An eagle person will seek the gifts of the West, North, and South.

Bear people from the West are introspective. They tend to run the same ideas over and over again in their mind. Bear people have the ability to look within themselves but become so occupied with inner realities that they fail to see, understand, and touch the external world. They must seek the remaining powers to achieve harmony and balance.

To determine which of the four powers were innate and which ones were to be acquired, the adult Indians carefully evaluated the children's behavior and their accounts of dreams and visions. When the child reached adolescence, the elders had an accurate understanding of his beginning place on the Medicine Wheel. They constructed a shield depicting the young person's beginning gift and the powers he must seek to become a whole person. Essentially, the shield was a map of the youth's consciousness that he carried everywhere and displayed for others to see. In this way, fellow seekers would know of each other's inherent strengths and weaknesses, and could help one another in their spiritual quest. The shields brought the Indian people together with a common philosophy and a common goal of living in harmony with every other thing in the Universe.[6]

There are many similarities between the Four Great Powers of the Medicine Wheel and the method of thought outlined by concentration-contemplation-meditation[7] (see Figure 20). Concentration corresponds to the gift of the South; meditation, the gift of the North. Contemplation involves both inductive and deductive reasoning. Inductive reason

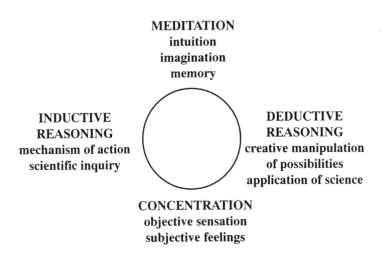

MEDITATION
intuition
imagination
memory

INDUCTIVE
REASONING
mechanism of action
scientific inquiry

DEDUCTIVE
REASONING
creative manipulation
of possibilities
application of science

CONCENTRATION
objective sensation
subjective feelings

Fig. 20. *There are many similarities between the Four Great Powers of the Medicine Wheel and the Rosicrucian method of concentration, contemplation (inductive and deductive reasoning), and meditation. Both systems can lead to that knowledge and wisdom permeating mystic experience.*

corresponds to the gift of the West. Deductive reasoning corresponds to the gift of the East. The Rosicrucian method of concentration, contemplation, and meditation is an orderly and holistic process of study that leads to that knowledge and wisdom which permeates mystic experience.

The American Indians discovered a universality for the symbol of the circle because of their close relationship with the forces of nature. The symbol of the circle provided them with a holistic understanding of their physical environment and a sense of immortality.

To the American Indian, everything the power of the world does is done in a circle. Black Elk, a holy man of the Oglala Sioux explains, "The sky is round, and I have heard that the Earth is round like a ball, and so are all the stars. The wind, in its greatest power, whirls. Birds make their nests in circles, for theirs is the same religion as ours. The sun comes forth and goes down again in a circle. The moon

Fig. 21. *The teachers among the Indians often constructed medicine wheels from stones or pebbles placed on the ground. Each stone represented one of the many things in the Universe. Thus, the wheel or circle represents the entire Universe.*

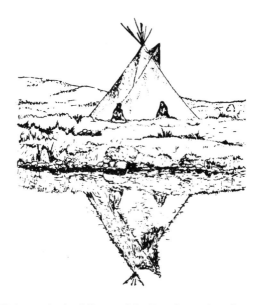

*"The Universe is the Mirror of the People, and each person is
a Mirror to every other person."*

does the same, and both are round. Even the seasons form a
great circle in their great changing, and always come back
again to where they were. The life of a man is a circle from
childhood to childhood, and so it is in everything where
power moves. Our tepees were round like the nests of birds,
and these were always set in a circle, the nation's hoop, a
nest of many nests, where the Great Spirit meant for us to
hatch our children."[8]

The movements of nature were circular long before the
arrival of mankind. When man arrived, his consciousness
reflected the glories of the universe, revealing to him the
concept or symbol of the circle. This symbol reflected back
into the external world in the form of practical applications

such as the tepee, the wheel, and a working knowledge of the cycles of nature. Then many ancient cultures such as the American Indian applied the symbol of the circle to gain an understanding of man's inner world. The circle became a guide to personal understanding of the nature of man, and man's place in nature.

EXERCISING THE IMAGINATION

The use of imagination and its faculty for symbolic thinking is essential to those desiring Mastery in Self, wholeness, and an experience of the Marriage of the Mind. The use of symbol, like the circle, can become a way of life, a way of perceiving and integrating experiences, a way of thinking, a way of wholeness and health.

The creation of those conditions conducive to harmony and balance is of paramount importance to the development of the mystic. For this reason the Rosicrucian student learns to balance correctly what he eats and drinks with how he breathes and thinks. The Rosicrucian student endeavors to eat a balanced diet, charges the water he drinks, and regularly uses breathing exercises. He further enhances the positive qualities of his personality with constructive, imaginative thinking and meditating. He also plans for adequate rest, sleep, and exercise.

The Rosicrucian system for attaining harmony and good health is not new. Some of the ancient Egyptian, Greek, and Roman mystic philosophers had similar formulas for simultaneously developing mind and body. These venerables believed that the development of one aided the activity of the other, that exercise and physical activity could change the state of one's mind; and that conversely, mental and imaginative activity could change one's physical and athletic competence. Let us examine each of these suppositions and observe what basis there may be for this point of view.

Throughout the ages there have been many subjective reports of connections between personality and physical fitness. Stereotypes of the athletic personality have often resulted. Some observers see the athlete as highly competitive, others see him or her as insensitive or even brutal; athletes are said to be fair, sportsman-like, masculine, arrogant, genteel, or immature, depending on whose assessment is taken. In fact, studies indicate that football coaches even stereotype players in terms of what position they play based on supposed personality characteristics, despite personality-test findings that show no relationship between position and personality. It seems that such stereotypes are more related to the observer's experiences with various athletes than to personality factors.

There are a number of reports, however, that demonstrate differences between the personalities of athletes and nonathletes. These studies indicate that on the average athletes tend to have high levels of leadership qualities, initiative, sense of personal worth, social maturity, self-confidence, and intellectual efficiency. For instance. personality studies at West Point Academy indicated that West Point athletes were more social, dominant, enthusiastic, adventuresome, tough-minded, group-oriented, and sophisticated than nonathletes at the same institution. The Cureton-Heusner study of Olympic champions indicated that these champions tended to be more intelligent, emotionally stable, dominant, venturesome, and much more self-assured than others. They also tended to disregard rules and reject group standards. Despite some differences and divergence in the findings of these and other studies, all seem to conclude that the physically fit person tends to be more emotionally stable, extraverted, and self-assured than his inactive counterpart.

While on the surface such studies seem to demonstrate a relationship between physical fitness and personality, some important questions remain. First, there is the fundamental problem of cause and effect. The personality of the athlete may be interpreted as a direct effect of his physical condition and participation in athletics. His personality may be said to be an effect, to some degree, of the special high-pressure social and psychological environment of competitive athletics. Or, on the other hand, personality traits may be a *cause* of success in athletics, not an *effect*. The person with certain personality traits will be attracted to athletics

	HIGH-FITNESS		LOW-FITNESS	
FACTOR	BEFORE	AFTER	BEFORE	AFTER
emotional stability	6.4	6.1	4.6	5.4
imagination	7.3	7.2	5.3	6.1
guilt-proneness	4.2	4.1	5.4	6.1
self-sufficiency	6.5	6.6	6.4	8.0

Table 6. *The Catteal 16 Personality Factor Questionnaire evaluates the intensity of 16 major personality source traits or individual personality factors, rating each on a ten-point scale. A score on any factor must be higher than 6 or lower than 4 to be considered significantly "high" or "low." Of the 16 personality factors, Ismail found that exercises influenced emotional stability, imagination, guilt, and self-sufficiency.*

while those who lack these traits will drop out. In support of this latter view, research indicated that personality traits vary among different sports and especially between persons in individual sports versus persons in team sports. Other complications arise, though, from the fact that these studies either dealt with adolescents having malleable personalities or with sports stars at the peak of their careers. Hence, these studies do not prove that exercise can change personality or influence the mind, and they do not reveal what is cause and what is effect.

Professor A. H. Ismail at Purdue University in a recent study may have laid to rest some of these criticisms. He administered the Cattell 16 Personality Inventory (see Table 6) to middle-aged participants before a physical-fitness program, and then again four months later. The fitness program consisted of the numbers 1 1/2 hours three times a week of group calisthenics, supervised running and a period of either swimming or team sports. Twenty-eight participants were divided into two groups of fourteen depending on high or low physical fitness at the start of the training period. Physical fitness criteria consisted of: exercise heart rate, percent lean body mass, maximal oxygen intake corrected by lean body mass, submaximal minute volume of ventilation corrected by body weight and resting diastolic blood pressure.

A comparison of personality factors at the start showed that the high-fitness group had significantly higher scores only on emotional stability and imagination.

A second comparison of personality factors at the conclusion of the program revealed that the low-fitness group's score on emotional stability had increased so markedly that there no longer was a significant difference between the two groups on that factor. A high score on this factor is associated with emotional maturity, calmness, the ability to perceive reality accurately despite emotional involvement, and with restraint in avoiding difficulties; low scores show a tendency to be affected by feelings and are somewhat related to, but not identical with general neuroticism. The low fitness group's score also showed increased imaginativeness, but as a group they still were not as strong as the high-fitness group. Imagination is a subtle trait. People in the high imaginative factor seemed to have an intense subjective and inner mental life; they are often described as unconventional, absorbed in ideas, enthralled by inner creations, and are generally enthusiastic.

Self-sufficiency was greatly increased in the low-fitness groups even beyond that of the high-fitness group. High scores in self-sufficiency indicate resourcefulness and introversion, and such a person is likely to be resolute and accustomed to making his own decisions. The low-fitness group also demonstrated a modest increase in proneness to guilt which may have been due either to guilt at taking time away from usual business activities or guilt at being confronted with the problem of physical unfitness.

While it may be difficult to explain all these changes and differences, two broad interpretations are immediately apparent. There can be a direct physical effect and benefit of conditioning due to exercise, such as in increased blood circulation to the brain, and there can be a psychological effect on personality which may be the result of setting, meeting, and conquering goals. Finally, both of these factors may interact with, reinforce, and facilitate each other.

Ismail's study confirms what exercise enthusiasts have claimed for thousands of years: that physical activity can rapidly change the state of one's mind, and that the effect on the mind can be of greater importance and benefit than simply the value of exercise to the body. This study implies that in only three months one can improve self-confidence, stability, and imagination by means of physical activity. But what about the reverse condition? Can proper use of the imagination, mental stability, and self-confidence increase athletic prowess?

Many research studies in recent years have demonstrated the value of visualizing or mental practice of an upcoming situation or the symbolic rehearsal of a physical activity in the absence of any gross muscular movement. The classic experiment regarding mental practice was reported by Australian psychologist Alan Richardson concerning the effects of visualization on free-throw scores of basketball players. The study involved three groups of students chosen at random, none of whom had ever practiced visualization.

The first group practiced making free-throws every day for twenty days. The second group made free-throws on the first and twentieth days, with no practice in between. The third group also made free-throws on the first and last days, but, in addition, they spent twenty minutes a day *imagining* sinking baskets. As in the external world, when these students mentally missed, they tried to correct their aim on the next shot. The first group, who actually practiced, improved 24% between the first and last day. The second group, who had done no practice of any kind, did not improve at all. The third group, who visualized throwing the ball through the basket, improved 23%. Similar studies involving dart throwing and other motor activities show the same kind of result.

Richardson noted that vividness of imagery among the mental practicers is less important than their ability to control the image. In other words, for visualizers to benefit from mental practice, it is not necessary for their image to be as real as life, but it is important for them to be able to *picture each part* of the free-throw. Richardson also concluded (as did the ancient Rosicrucians) that mental practice is more effective if the visualizer "feels" as well as "sees" the activity he is symbolically practicing. For example, a person picturing free-throws would have better results if he "felt" the ball in his hands and "heard" the ball bounce, as well as "saw" the ball drop through the basket.

Many professional athletes, in thinking over their reasons for success, have realized the importance of holding images in the mind. A number of athletes have written books about and developed whole teaching systems based on visualization. Alex Morrison in his book *Better Golf Without Practice* says a person must have a clear mental image of the correct swing, and be able to visualize it, before he can do it successfully. Ben Hogan has described mentally rehearsing each shot, "feeling" the club head striking the ball, and "feeling" himself follow through in the correct manner. Johnny Bulla, another professional golfer, believed in picturing the end result. He instructed people to see mentally their ball dropping in the cup, to know that it would happen.

In *The Inner Game of Tennis* W. Timothy Gallwey instructs people to picture hitting the ball where they want it to go and then let it happen (in Rosicrucian terminology this is called *release*):

> ... stand on the base line, breathe deeply a few times and relax. Look at the can [target for the exercise]. Then visualize the path of the ball from your racket to the can. See the ball hitting the can right on the label. If you like, shut your eyes and imagine yourself serving and the ball hitting the can. Do this several times. If in your imagination the ball misses the can, that's all right; repeat the image a few times until the ball hits the target. Now take no thought of how you should hit the ball. Don't try to hit the target. Ask your body . . . to do whatever is necessary to hit the can, then let it do it. Exercise no control; correct for no imagined bad habits. Having programmed yourself with the desired flight of the ball, simply trust your body to do it.

Studies show that imaginative mental practice can improve self-confidence. But not only does visualization increase confidence, it also directly effects muscles. In his experiments the physiologist Edmund Jacobson showed that a person's muscles demonstrated small (invisible) but detectable amounts of electrical activity associated with movement when that person imagined a specific activity. Thus, a person may develop muscle memory of an activity and better coordination simply by imagining that activity, as well as by engaging in it.

What is apparent from studies such as these is not only that the mind's activities affect the body and the body's activities affect the mind, but that both reinforce each other. The process of visualization and release is the key, for it is human imagination that allows the interaction of both body and mind. Both physical and mental exercise give us the opportunity to use and develop our imagination. Learning to rely on the Inner Self and the conditions which the Inner Self can imagine and direct is what builds self-confidence, emotional stability, and self-assurance.

The Rosicrucian principles of visualization, release, and inner experience can be broadly applied in every aspect of our daily life. Better physical condition and improved personality characteristics are but examples of what can result from such application. The principles, the process, and the technique are limited only by our imagination.

IMAGINATION AND THE HEALING MIND

The use of symbolic thinking and psychic energization techniques for physical health and healing dates back to well before the rise of experimental science. In fact, visualization may be the oldest healing technique employed by the ancients. The earliest records of such techniques are found on cuneiform slabs from Babylonia and Sumeria, and on temple walls and papyri of ancient Egypt. We might assume that there were antecedents for these techniques among ancient aboriginal tribes. These techniques may still be practiced among the aboriginal tribes today. The practice of the healing art in these tribes centers around their shamans, special members of the tribe who are believed to have the power to heal diseases. Shamans can believe they are in contact with tribal spirits through dreams, visions, and mystical experiences—that is, through forms of symbolic thinking and visualization. Shamans heal through symbolic ceremonies and rituals in which disease-causing, malevolent spirits are symbolized, imaged, and confronted by images of a powerful, positive force. By this means, the power of the malevolent spirit is dissipated. The mask (or persona) is the concrete form of a shaman's spiritual visualization.

Ancient civilizations used symbolic thinking in similar ways. In Egypt, Babylonia, and Assyria, people believed illness was caused by evil spirits. Treatment constituted an appeal to the deities to exorcise a demon from the patient. Special priests acted as diagnosticians and interpreted signs from the sun and storm gods. Significantly, these priests referred to their own dreams. The patient also might be encouraged to receive a healing dream by sleeping in the temple.

Ancient Greek, Indian, and Oriental civilizations used techniques for healing similar to the Egyptian and Babylonian ones. In their healing ceremonies, the magician-priest would perform incantations and prayers, and also use dreams, herbal remedies, and devices invested with magic. In these healing systems, disease, visualized in the image of a demon, was exorcised by a figure of authority, a physician-priest. That figure derived authority from his ability to visualize an infinitely higher authority, a spirit, or god. Therefore, the god was believed to heal through the priests.

However, evolving alongside this authoritative mode of healing was a more subjective, mystical philosophy based on people experiencing their own imagery and the flow of psychic energies within themselves. This mystical tradition permeated the thought of Hermetic philosophers in Egypt, Platonic philosophers in Greece, Sufis in Persia, and Buddhists and Hindus in India and the Orient. In the Middle Ages in Europe it expressed itself in the mysticism of Christian Gnostics, Jewish Qabbalists, and the secret mystical orders like the Rosicrucians.

The philosophers in these groups held in common a symbolic image of a spiritual center which formed the universe. They believed that this symbolic center could be touched by individuals through their use of visualization and meditation. These philosophers held images that supported their belief in the primacy of spirit over matter, of mind over body; they believed that matter is a manifestation of spirit. They believed that symbolic thinking could manifest itself as either health or disease in the body. Just as a skill in basketball or tennis can be improved through the use of inner rehearsals in visualization and meditation, so too the body can respond to attitude and symbolic imagery in matters of health. In modern terms, then, what is symbolically experienced in the mind can have profound effects in the body.

The modern basis of Rosicrucian health and healing instruction draws heavily on the Nodin manuscript. This instruction dates from about A.D. 1350. However, the material which it presented is far older than that date, possibly going back to the time of Plato, Anaxagoras, and Plotinus of Greece, and the Hermetic tradition of Egypt. In essence it says: there is One creative force in the universe, a divine mind. This creative force or Divine Mind is of a vibratory nature and it separates into a positive and negative polarity. The image conveyed by the Nodin manuscript is of this Vital Source streaming to us through our Sun, although it was thought that the actual force coming through our Sun originated in a far more remote area, a central universal source. Rosicrucian studies go into great detail concerning the operations of these two polarities.

A balance of these two aspects is experienced in the body as harmonium. Harmonium manifests as vital, vibrant health. From the Rosicrucian concept, a lack of harmonium or disharmony is an imbalance between these two aspects, and this imbalance permits the condition of disease or ill health to arise and manifest. In this view, ill health has its beginning in the psychic or immaterial part of man. To the Rosicrucian harmony is thus paramount to the healing processes. Once harmony is disrupted, the Rosicrucian works on balancing the positive and negative aspects. The positive polarity in the body is enhanced by imaginative thinking, a positive attribute of Mind, and by breathing air. Negative polarity is given to the body by the material elements of the Earth taken into it, by the eating of proper food and by the drinking of water. When the individual learns to balance correctly what he eats and drinks with how he breathes and thinks, Rosicrucians have observed that harmony and health is experienced.

There is also another law that Rosicrucians associate with the subconscious mind and the process of visualization. It states that when a final stage or end result is visualized or suggested, the subconscious mind finds the means for carrying out the directive. Usually the subconscious means is by way of the autonomic nervous system. This process is a double-edged sword, for it also means that with self-images containing negative elements of fear, frustration, and depression we create our own discontent and poor health. In chronic disease the process is intensified as the patient comes to believe that he will never be able to overcome his poor condition. Essentially then, the Rosicrucian path of healing outlined in the Nodin manuscript implies that we ourselves are responsible for the conditions of our life, and that if we are to secure health and harmony we must first master ourselves and attain self-reliance.

To summarize what we have said so far: What the mind imagines can have a strong influence upon the body. This directive influence can be either constructive or destructive; it can raise us up to our highest potential, or it can pull us down into the depths of illness and despair. The choice of image is ours.

Medieval alchemists believed that the impure body and mind could be purified of negative imagery and conditions. Purification involves separation of the different symbolic images in a person's consciousness. Some alchemists may have used the chemical metaphor to represent mental transmutation. The image of a substance or part of the body becoming purer and purer is an ancient and very potent healing visualization.

The alchemist known as Paracelsus was a Renaissance physician whose medicine embodied the link between mysticism and science. Paracelsus worked in the early 1500's in Switzerland. He is considered the father of modern drug therapy and scientific medicine. Nevertheless, Paracelsus opposed the idea of separating the soul or vital essence from the healing process. Like many Rosicrucians before and after him, Paracelsus advocated what today is referred to as holistic healing. Among his medical theories, Paracelsus held that imagination and faith were the cause of natural phenomena, that imagination produces disease in humans and animals, and it may cure them. To Paracelsus, imagination is the creative power in man.

Since Paracelsus' time mental and physical methods of healing have divided into two distinct systems. Medical approaches in the form of drug therapy and surgery have grown to be the dominant authoritative treatment in the West. Yet, traditions of mental healing have also continued. Since 1900 attempts to integrate the two separate approaches have appeared and explorations of the mind's role in healing have been made. Physicians have long recognized the efficacy of the placebo, a substance having no known pharmacological action, yet which may still work in both physical and mental conditions. In one placebo study patients hospitalized with bleeding ulcers showed a lasting 70% improvement when the doctors gave them an injection of distilled water and assured them that it was a new medication that would cure them. The patients' expectations played a strong part in effecting relief from their symptoms. In another study patients were given a drug that normally induces vomiting and nausea. But patients were told that the drug would stop the symptoms of nausea and vomiting they were already experiencing, and it did!

One may postulate that even a placebo, or ineffective drug, can become a symbol of healing. It is as if the symbol triggers in the patient a subconscious, healing image that produces a healing. The fact that the drug symbol has been administered to the patient by a doctor lends authority to the patient's own visualization of the drug's healing effectiveness.

Many of us may experience examples of body and mind interaction in our own daily lives. For example, when we are frightened, our body responds with an increased heart-rate, more rapid breathing, "butterflies" in our stomach, and increased sweating. These reactions are called the *fight or flight response*. These reactions ready the body for action by stimulating the sympathetic division of the autonomic nervous system and the adrenal glands. In fact, whenever we perceive a threat in either our inner or outer world, our body will be ready to fight or run.

Blushing and sexual arousal are other common examples of a body response to stimuli perceived in our mind. Our body reacts regardless of whether the stimulation has occurred in the external world or is an image held in the mind.

Just as we have experienced fear and other forms of excitation, we also experience feelings associated with relaxation. These subtle feelings are the result of parasympathetic activation, and include slowing of the heart rate, slowing of breathing, and lack of tension in skeletal muscles.

During relaxation almost every cell in the body can participate by reducing its metabolism. This is reflected in a 13% reduction in oxygen consumption. In contrast, during sleep oxygen consumption only decreases by 5%. Blood lactate levels are also reduced and continue at low levels for hours afterward. This is significant because in high concentrations, blood lactate is associated with anxiety.

Chronic stress and strong, negative emotions such as fear, anxiety, anger, desperation, despair, and even more subtle forms of chronic anger as impatience, irritation, grief and disappointment, can all lead to stress diseases such as hypertension, heart and auto-immune diseases. Relaxation can reduce chronic stress and susceptibility to such diseases. Symbolic healing images are enhanced by states of deep relaxation where we have let go of anger and fear. The state of relaxation in itself may also contribute to the creation of harmony, balancing active and receptive qualities of life experience.

Besides affecting body physiology and metabolism, relaxation, visualization, and symbolic thinking can affect the electric and magnetic energy fields surrounding the body. For instance, people have a negative electric potential of 3 to 10 millivolts between the left and right side of the body. While relaxing, visualizing, and working with symbolic images, there is a balancing effect with this potential gradient dropping to -1 mv or less. Conversely, mental anxiety, stress, illness, or trauma can raise these potential gradients to above -20 mv. High potentials are initiated in response to injury and are lowered as repair is completed.

The practicing Rosicrucian student uses both electromagnetic and vital energies in conjunction with healing visualizations and symbolic imagery. The understanding of self-transformation is an ancient study, and continues to occupy the minds of those seeking an understanding of harmony and peace, and a deeper knowledge of Self.

IMAGINATION: IN PRACTICE

Neuropsychobiology has been referred to as one of the last frontiers of human endeavor. The idea of comprehending how our own mind and brain works is too compelling to resist. This seems to hold true whether we examine the physical mechanisms for objective and subjective reception of sense perceptions and feelings; or whether we look at the mental faculty of discrimination with its deductive and inductive reason by which we evaluate ideas and perceptions; or whether we look beyond the physical and mental, to the "higher" faculty of imagination supported by its dual elements of memory and intuition.

By this "higher" faculty of imagination, memory, and intuition, we are able to visualize. We can comprehend, create, and transform ideas and images, as well as manifest these conditions and attitudes as a harmony either in the

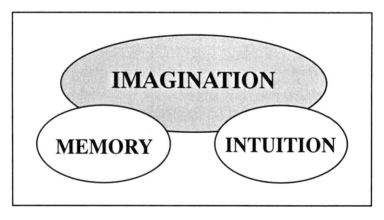

mind, the body, or our world. We do this by plunging deep into the pool of our subconscious memory and then bringing to the surface of imagination our slippery thoughts, images, and ideals. While we reflect upon the imaged thought caught in the mirrored surface of imagination, the intuition can descend to penetrate, to inspire, to inflame this thought into new and transcendent forms.

The intuition is silent and invisible; the observer, we who are reflecting in imagination, may only perceive that our ideas and thoughts seem to take on a life of their own; that as we reflect or visualize, the images grow and mature as of themselves, bringing with them harmonious and startling changes, and bearing a many-colored fruit which transports the observer to an ever-greater insight, understanding, wisdom, and good health. With use and practice, we can develop our capacities for employing memory, imagination, and intuition, and thus come to experience the harmony present in our inner and outer worlds.

CHAPTER 8

CREATIVE EXPRESSION

SOURCE AND ACTION OF CREATIVITY

P oets, artists, and creative people of all kinds receive ideas through subconscious and symbolizing functions of the mind. For instance, during a receptive state a writer may experience a "relaxed attention" or a "relaxed anticipation" and then also feel "the ideas just came to me." Some poets feel that their poetic images arise from their subconscious, while others feel that the images come from outside themselves. Some ancient people symbolized the source of ideas as a goddess or a muse, and in some cases as a daemon, a genie, or the *Entheos,* that is, the *God Within.*

Regardless of the ultimate source of creative ideas, the creative process itself has often been observed to consist of four stages. The four-stage theory of creativity is prevalent in many mystical schools and is widely accepted by scholars in the field of creativity. In the modern world, these four stages are thought to be based on the accounts of famous people's creative experiences, but there are analogous descriptions in the four creative worlds of the medieval *Qabalah,* the *Paut Netura* of the ancient Egyptians, and in the Thought Process discussed in this book.

In the first stage of creative experience people observe, consciously collect data, ideas, and techniques, and methodically file away potential images. In this first stage they get together the tools and raw materials that seem potentially

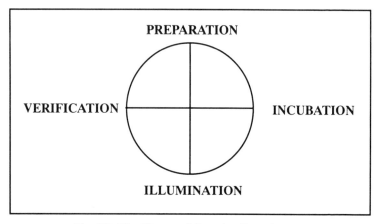

Fig. 22. *The Phases of Creative Experience.*

applicable to the creative challenges they are facing. During this preparatory stage a person's mood can often be that of excitement and perplexity.

The second stage of creative experience can be called *incubation.* In this stage, creative people "release" or "let go" their conscious hold on the problem. They may rest, relax, or turn their attention in another direction. During this stage images in the subconscious shift and realign themselves. This is the critical stage in creativity. In the incubation stage writers may get sudden glimpses of parts of the solution they are seeking.

The third stage can be called *illumination.* The solution or inspiration most often spontaneously occurs in this stage of illumination, often at an unexpected moment, usually accompanied by feelings of certainty and joy. In the brain, the limbic system is responsible for, first, the sensory aspects of the experience of illumination (sometimes described literally as a sensation of a light going on), and second, for the experience of certainty. As one creative person puts it, "I simply know that I know." This is the moment of discovery; the moment when the writer sees the complete outline of a new composition or a poet records the central lines of a new poem. There is a sense of unity and wholeness as all the separate parts come together in a new and cohesive form.

The fourth and final stage can be called *verification* or *revision*. In this stage writers work out the details and make the ideas manifest in a form or structure. Like the first stage this is a stage of keen observation, of effort and skill. But whereas in the first stage ideas and techniques are gathered, in the fourth stage they are employed. Verification, like preparation, is largely felt to be a conscious process. However, in the stage of verification the imagined image is like an invisible mold onto which we superimpose and manifest content and technique.

For a scientist, this last stage involves organizing the data and even conducting experiments which will prove, illustrate, and demonstrate his theory. For a sculptor this stage can involve solving the technical problems of pouring the bronze and polishing the finished product. For a writer or a poet it also means dealing with matters of technique and polish. Has the writer used the very best word to convey the idea and force of emotion behind the idea? Have needless words been omitted, ie., adverbs and adjectives? Is each sentence tailored, precise, and contributory to the purpose of the whole? Is the idea complete? Does the ending complete the beginning? Or, are there missing parts, breaks yet to be meditated upon, visualized, and brought to completion?

To summarize what has been said so far, the creative ideas for our writing, as well as the creative development of new or appropriate writing techniques will be found in the subconscious mind following an appropriate period of incubation. To this process then, the incubation stage is the most important one, although the stages of preparation, illumination, and verification are also essential. The creative idea will come to consciousness (be born following the proper incubation) in a moment of illumination. This moment is thought to take place in a psychic state of "nonordinary" or "altered" consciousness.

Meditation or an openness to symbolic thinking is a means of putting ourselves into this receptive state of mind—specifically becoming aware of images arising out of the subconscious. In terms of creativity, the images experienced are unique forms of images or relationships that the subconscious mind transforms or transmutes in its natural tendency to resolve our perception of problems. By means of such transformations of attitude, outlook, and reality, we can come to experience the order and the harmony present in the universe. The moment of illumination is in itself a mystical experience—a dense, wordless, sensory experience (variously filled with light, sound, smell, tactile and taste sensations) of a highly complicated concept.

As practiced by Rosicrucian students, creative visualization is also a technique of manifesting a definite future condition by producing its symptoms in the present. When we demonstrate the pattern of a condition in the present, we open possibilities for its unfoldment and full manifestation. In demonstrating a new pattern, we give direction to the unfoldment in our life. We are initiating a condition which can lead to surprises and vivid experiences.

Decide on something you would like to be such as the kind of creative writer that is already a seed within you. How do you feel as a creative writer? Feeling this way, what actions do you see yourself taking? What abilities and skills does this creative writer, which is you, manifest? How does this creative writer do what he or she does? Then ask yourself how you already do similar or analogous things in other aspects of your life. If both you and others are doing similar kinds of things then there must be a universal principle involved. When you identify the principle, you will suddenly find that you can more easily apply it to your writing just as you already apply it to other aspects of your life.

In other words, in preparation we decide on something we would like to be. We outline the symptoms and characteristics of that "being." Then we "let go" of the details. In illumination we let the visualization of the outline as a "whole" come to us and we feel what it would be like to be a whole person exhibiting the characteristics of this type of creativity. Then we validate our inner experience. We behave in a manner which indicates to us that we are indeed the kind of person or being that we visualized. We can assume the characteristics and feelings of our inner experience in everyday life. We can use our outline to guide our actions and reactions, and, even more, we can "relive" our intuitive feelings. If we fall away from our vision or forget to "feel" the way a master writer-craftsman feels, we do not have to berate ourself. We can simply observe, learn, and refocus our attention on the guiding vision and "inner feeling" which we experienced in our visualizations and meditations. As a silent observer, we can simply watch to see how soon we become as we set out to be.

When we are truly seeking to improve ourselves, then we are really living! The essence of life is insight, creativity, originality, and flux. Nothing, not even oneself, remains the same. This is the beauty of existence. As we learn to use our full psychic awareness and move our lives into harmony with each circumstance we encounter in life, we discover that we are privileged to experience the ever-new, exciting motion of the Cosmic. We are all cosmic instruments and have the capacity to demonstrate that instrumentality. Changes that we experience within ourselves, in our thinking, and in the way we feel about ourselves, also reflect outside our lives, too.

If you want to be a writer, then be a writer *now*. Assume now the characteristics of a writer. Write! Do not be concerned with what you write, just write, write and write some more. The more you write without judgment and self-criticism during this initial creative stage, the more you will learn about writing and about yourself. Before long you will be writing more and more what needs to be written and you will become an ever-more effective agent of cosmic harmony. Your creative thought, your creative solutions, and your creative activities will in themselves create harmony in your world.

In living the creative life, we advance on a journey that shows us new ways to live, new ways to think, and new ways to respond. The creativity and originality that you will demonstrate as a writer will take hold of the core of your being and prepare your higher faculties of mind for real enjoyment and satisfaction. Your own awareness, imagination, and attunement are your vehicles for reaching your personal destination. Truly, the imaginative power of visualization, release, and inner experience can be broadly applied in every aspect of daily life, yet even if you only creatively prepare, incubate, illuminate, and apply these principles in one aspect of your life, you will still have effects on your whole life and world.

EVOKING OUR CREATIVE POWER

When we participate in creative processes, we can explore countless numbers of possible patterns before finally settling on an idea. Many of us, however, encounter emotional resistance to the flow of creative possibilities. We demand of our minds an immediate, logical, finished product that stifles creative exploration. Most of us do not lack ideas. What we lack is a rapid and direct means of getting in touch with those ideas. Is there a magic key for unlocking those secret reservoirs of imaginative power?

One magic key described by Gabriele Rico[1] is a creative process called *clustering*. A similar process using patterns is termed *mind mapping* by Tony Buzan.[2] Both techniques use the right brain's ability to image and synthesize. Clustering and mind mapping temporarily suspend the normally dominant left-brain activity that is logical and orderly. These are non-linear brain-storming processes akin to free association. Invisible ideas become visible, flashing out in lightning-like associations that allow new patterns of ideas to emerge.

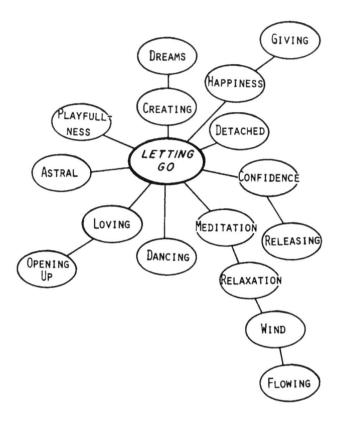

Fig. 23. *Dena's Cluster and vignette.* "*Letting go means being detached from life's pressures and personal problems so I can have a better perspective on people and situations—finding happiness in giving, no matter how small or insignificant. It means creating in my mind the dreams that I may at times find out of reach or feel underserving of. Letting go means playfulness by not taking life's burdens too seriously and knowing that there is also humor. I should take time out to feed my soul with laughter, loving, and dancing. These things will open me up to have another perspective in life. In letting go I may find my answers through meditation. When I do this I am totally relaxed. I become like the wind. My burdens are behind me and I feel light and free. My astral body has no boundaries or limitations. I flow easily towards a better understanding.*"—Dena

Initially, thinkers accustomed to a logical, step-by-step approach find clustering unsettling. A frequently made remark is, "This is crazy. Where is this taking me?" With experience, however, most thinkers eventually discover that they can explore creative ideas without first knowing the "who, what, where, why, and when." They find that creative exploration is a practical, exciting, and ultimately inspiring adventure.

In one Rose-Croix University class, students were introduced to the clustering process. The students drew a circle in the center of a clean page. In this circle they placed a "seed" or "nuclear" idea. Then they opened themselves to any thoughts, ideas, images, feelings, or emotions that this "seed" evoked. In their case the "seed" idea was the principle of "letting go." Ideas associated with "letting go" made a splash in the students' minds and were quickly jotted down on the paper and circled, with the circled ideas radiating outward from the "seed" idea like ripples in a pool (see figures 23 and 24). Some associations triggered other associations, and new circles radiated out from the secondary ideas. These secondary ideas often spread to yet other associations in a continuous, rapidly expanding ripple effect. (For a step-by-step explanation of the clustering process, please see Appendix 3.)

In clustering, each association leads inevitably to the next with a connection of its own even though the analytical left brain may not perceive the logic. These sudden subconscious associations make the connections that create the marvelous complexity of images and their rich emotional qualities. When captured on paper these associations either

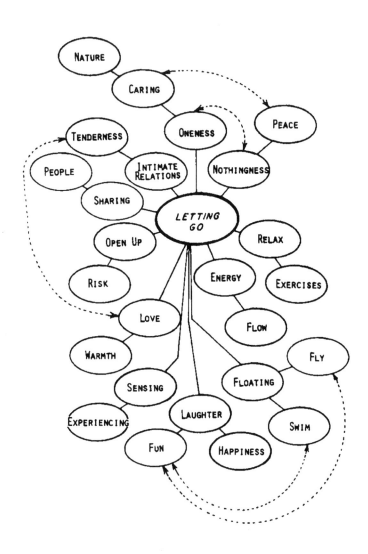

Fig. 24. *Kurt's Cluster.*

suddenly or gradually reveal new patterns and meanings arising from an apparent chaos.

Northrop Frye, the literary critic, observed that any principle or idea can become "a storm center of meanings, sounds and associations radiating out indefinitely like ripples in a pool."

⇦ Fig. 24. *"Letting go means I feel warm inside, that I am able to love people as they are, and not as I expect or want them to be.*

"Let go and open up—risk. That is I what I am doing—being tender, playing, having intimate relationships, fun. I risk being turned down. I don't feel that is risky because I am letting the life energy flow outwards—through everybody, everything on its omnidirectional path.

"I let go and merge with life, with people—enjoying life, letting the creative impulses flow through me outwards towards the world, establishing resonance in others, opening them to the cosmic reality, to higher planes of being, of creativity and consciousness.

"I allow myself to stay in a feeling of nothingness and Peace Profound. I get energy and vitality by releasing my control over myself and others. I laugh, float, fly, and swim in a vibrant ocean of fun, joy, happiness, and spontaneity. My whole being is sensing and experiencing on all planes. I enjoy life at full throttle.

"I have—finally—awakened my sleepy right brain hemisphere and realize the untested and untasted possibilities. I have gone beyond my imagined limitations, jumped through the gray sticky clouds of illusion. I have set me free, taken the pink balloon, soared the sky, and further penetrated time and space. I am the cosmonaut of the past, present, and future, visiting worlds yet to be dreamed of. I play with forms, colors, and dimensions. I fly through black holes and watch God dissolving billions of solar systems, and admire Him when He is creating new and different worlds and universes out of the white at the other end of the black holes.

"I know not why I came here on earth: I should learn to let go, to enjoy life, and spread that joy, that Light, to every possible corner of the Earth. I AM now free, I have been born again. I died, but I have been resurrected, and am deeply thankful for that."—Kurt

Students find that clustering is rapid, the entire process taking only two to four minutes to reach new patterns, meanings, and insights. After the insight arises the student writes a brief vignette, a thumbnail sketch or cameo, of the insight. Writing the vignette which expresses the insight is also rapid, often taking no more than another five to ten minutes. As Frye suggests, clustering is like a thunderstorm: from the gathering of the clouds with the first ideas, to the clusters falling like a cloudburst, the lightning-flash insights, the clearing blue sky of the vignette, and the rainbow of the accomplishment—all in perhaps only fifteen minutes. The results are often surprising, sometimes even awesome. A frequent comment is, "It simply wrote itself!"

The two examples shown in Figures 23 and 24 are clearly impressive samples of creative writing. They were done by students who did not consider themselves professional writers. English is not the first language of the writer of the Figure 24 vignette. In fact, both authors felt that this was truly a first experience of creative writing for them—an initiation.

While human nature resists the unfamiliar and unconventional, once this resistance to using the clustering approach is overcome, people find this creative exploration of ideas exciting and surprisingly productive. Students use the process to take essay exams; businessmen and engineers for writing memos and reports; writers for developing ideas, the applications are limitless. For many RCU students the process produced enormous changes of attitude and tapped previously undiscovered personal creative powers. The process reveals that each of us possesses latent creative genius—

genius awaiting our release. Clustering can be a key for releasing our imaginative powers within.

Many of us encounter emotional resistance to change, to openness, to risk. Our problems and conflicts call out to us to change our old, safe ways of doing things. We often demand immediate, simple solutions and pat, logical answers. Such demands stifle self-exploration and growth.

In self-transformation we often explore countless feelings, memories, and fears before letting go of the past. How can Rosicrucian students learn to replace old habits and defensive behavior with openness to new growth and evolution? How can we tap the creative possibilities within and uncover inner truth?

A frater experienced major conflict in his reaction to a chronic illness. He had previously explored a number of approaches to resolving the conflict with limited success. The frater subsequently participated in a Mindquest experiment that employed techniques utilizing openness, inner exploration, and intuitive attunement. Through his exploration he gained new insights into his attitudes and the effects these had upon his life and the conflicts he was experiencing. These insights were particularly helpful in offering creative approaches to the resolution of his conflict. They increased his choice of effective and creative responses to his life situation, as he reports in Figure 25.

Sometimes we are unable to accomplish what we want. Many of us believe that change comes about through sheer exertion of will power. Sometimes, however, even great

(Continued on page 152)

Fig. 25. *Frater A's Vignette.*

When I think about my experience with illness I first recall the physical pain of trying to deal with sensory, muscular, and digestive faculties that progressively fail me; and more serious emotional pain of coping with rejection, loss of confidence, trust, esteem, ambition, enthusiasm, aliveness, joy, creativity, fulfillment of feeling I need protection and becoming closed, hard, cold, distant; losing the ability to learn about self and others, cutting off relationships; and finally, I recall the mental spiritual pain of feeling separate, isolated, alone, cut off from life and evolution, dead.

The cost seems so overwhelming that I think there can be no benefit to me in such disease. A little reflection shows me otherwise. The illness provides a battery of excuses for justifying what I want to do and avoiding what I don't. I can play it safe; I have an excuse for not communicating when I feel emotionally threatened. I have an excuse for pacifying the anger of others. I don't have to take responsibility for actions and behaviors. I can avoid the truth about myself or what I fear might be the truth. I can use the illness to control the behavior of others.

I can appear noble, I can persevere against impossible obstacles, even to the point of being a martyr. In doing the "impossible" I can feel superior, feel I ought to be admired, respected, accepted. I fear rejection. If I should happen to fail, I cannot be blamed. It's not my fault if fail to fulfill myself, my relationships, career and personal goals.

The question is not whether I should do my best, be creative, strive for excellence. The question is whether I will continue to play the noble role that is protected and safe, or choose to risk, to be open, soft, warm, compassionate, vulnerable, in order that I might explore the wholeness of my Self and others. To play a noble role is a drama that limits my sharing the whole or drama that limits my sharing the whole or genuine me. Moreover, the role I chose did not succeed in making me safe. I merely cast a cloak of illusory protection over that which needs no protection, which cannot be protected, and which, while covered, I cannot consciously explore.

To truly live, to let my light shine, to choose love and wholeness, is the way of risk, learning, test, trial, growth, evolution, enlightenment. This is the path of courage, the path of the unfolding Rose and Cross.

Let me realize how courageous I am to face fear, anger, sadness, grief; to face invisible bodily mutilations, illness, and even death; to face the beastliness of my own negative emotions. I am given the opportunity to meet my own soul, experience the preciousness of life, know the genuine confidence that comes only from trusting the vital forces of the Cosmic. No greater opportunity will ever come to me, and no greater courage will ever be called for than my meeting my own fear, my personal Terror on the Threshold, my own initiator.

I would have avoided fear and life's initiations. I would have separated myself from life by running away or dwelling in resentment and anger. Yet such emotions are merely the signpost that the initiator is at hand. Just beyond the threshold of illusory shadow and fear waits my Self, the reassurance I most desire.

As I meet the Terror, let me remember that I am enfolded with love and support. No matter what has happened to my body, I am still whole, and those whom I love are one with my wholeness. Oneness and separateness cannot co-exist. My mind's talk would say otherwise. But to behold a dream figure as sick, mutilated, and separate is no more actual than to regard it as healthy and beautiful. My experience of my Self is beautiful and whole.

I am a magnificent, wonder-filled human being privileged to share with all whom I love the essential qualities of soul that I project. I am whole and actual, and unity-actuality is not a thing of dreams.

My heart-light illumines the world. My just being here sharing light, trusting life, opening to love is a gift to all who would live and shine in love. I am grateful that I am beginning to allow life to give me this special gift of humility, knowledge of my human frailty, knowledge of the Light that I am radiating. I can radiate the truth about my Self: that I am not my body, drama, or disease; I am what we all are and what we tend to forget. I am the Light of the world and, radiating what I am, what every person is while in love, we all come to be a little more free.—Frater A.

efforts of will power are not enough. What do we do when attempts to change fail? Give up? Try harder, only to fail again? If we tie self-esteem to success, then giving up or even trying harder without success can erode self-esteem.

One way to accomplish breakthrough and change at such times is to understand and transmute the hidden motives that may keep us locked into our present behavior. At some time in our lives we may have put hidden, subconscious motives in place to protect ourselves from emotional pain, especially disapproval and rejection. When we are willing to face our hidden fears and protecting motives, we can pass over the threshold of fear and, through understanding, reach our inner light. For those willing to explore their feelings and fears, deeper understanding of self (and Self!) and change can naturally and gradually come about.

Visualization and meditation are two techniques that many people use to explore subjective and subconscious feelings. Such explorations often provide new understanding of the hidden motivations that govern much of our behavior. Frater A found the clustering process, which applies visualization and meditation techniques, particularly helpful in exploring his subconscious motivations and subjective feelings. The clustering process itself has been described as a tool for creative expression, but many have also found that the clustering process can assist in our exploring Self. Self-exploration often leads to change, a sense of freedom, and increased self-esteem.

Another subject experienced frequent feelings of sadness triggered by difficulty in relationships. He wanted to let go of mood swings and experience more harmony and peace. Previous attempts to change this pattern were only temporarily successful. Life incidents continued to trigger feelings of sadness and emotional swings. He then applied the cluster process to this issue, using "sadness" as the nucleus. As his cluster and vignette (see Figure 26) show, the process brought him a deeper understanding of sadness and of himself, his feelings and behavior. The frater saw how his sadness affects his life and his relationships. He found that he could choose to change his attitudes, resulting in a stabilization of his moods, improved self-esteem and self-confidence, and increased rapport with others. He now felt more centered, receptive to life, and others were more receptive and responsive to him.

Through such self-exploration many people learn to overcome personal fear, superstitious beliefs, and ignorance—self-imposed obstacles to joy, harmony, and Peace Profound. The clustering process is one means of making self-explorations and keeping a record of our adventures and transformations (also see Chapter Four).

The physical practice of creating the cluster pattern allows us to assume to the Inner Self in a free, yet substantive manner. Each succeeding element in the cluster stimulates new associations, unfolding and revealing the content of portions of the subconscious or unconscious often seemingly unavailable to our outer, objective consciousness. The patterns that these elements form and the connections they make can trigger an awareness of associations previously unnoticed or overlooked by our outer mind.

Both fratres applied the clustering process in a practical and creative manner to specific areas of concern in their lives. The process could be further expanded by using an element of the primary cluster as the nucleus or seed of another cluster and repeating the procedure. An insight gained from the vignette could also become the seed for an expanded cluster. Other creative approaches could include comparing or linking clusters on related topics as well as the associated vignettes.

Further insights can be gained by reviewing the cluster pattern at a later date and writing a new or revised vignette. The same technique applies to reviewing the vignette as well. Such reviews can also provide benchmarks for our progress, growth, and evolution.

While clustering can provide fresh insights and breakthroughs, it is well to remember that untangling the subtle

---

Fig. 26. *"Sadness puts up a wall between other people and me.* ⇨ *I withdraw, often not even noticing it. Other people see it and can't get through the wall. I feel closed off, but am really keeping people at arm's length.*

"When I let go, it allows the love and peace and centeredness I feel to come out, and it does come out. I can then 'come out.' When I let go and come out, I am there for myself and there for others.

"It is not necessary to 'figure out' the sadness—it is just an attachment. Acknowledge the feeling, then release it—let go. The love and centeredness and peace are the truth, the actuality, that the illusion of sadness, separateness, loneliness, loss or lack try to hide. The sadness is a barrier or wall, but letting go shows that the wall is equally illusory.

"When I let go, the peace and love and harmony, the wellness, wholeness, wholesomeness, centeredness just well up and fill me and flow over into all my life and out to others. We can be saints. I can be a saint. Sadness is just an attachment. It is time to let it go. As I do, I feel the Peace and Love within come out, lighten me up, light me up."
—Namasté

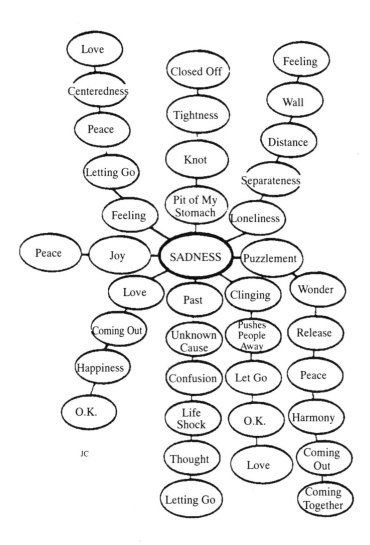

Fig. 26. *Frater B's Cluster and Vignette.*

web of issues and fears contained in some of our emotional conflicts can sometimes take years. In the first years of the 20th century, Dr. H. Spencer Lewis made a significant injunction: "Not through revolution but evolution are all things accomplished in time." Tools such as the cluster process can assist us to initiate change. Through persistence and application we can continuously change and evolve. This persistence, however, includes such attitudes as a willingness to evolve, build and reinforce new responses, new unfolding awareness, and an openness to continuous growth. Knowledge and technique are only the beginning. Our doing the exercise is an initiation. The application of knowledge brings wisdom and transformation, essential steps in manifesting our Mastery in Self.

CLUSTERING FOR ENLIGHTENMENT

To become as a walking question mark is a goal of the Rosicrucian student. The Rosicrucian student wants his or her understanding of every word, law, and principle in life demonstrated and made so plain and simple that he can demonstrate that law to himself and others in appropriate circumstances.

To ask, to question old beliefs is the first step in the acquisition of knowledge and wisdom. To question what it might mean to us to be a "walking question mark" could also be a step towards understanding the wisdom of the Rosicrucian Path. Consequently, people throughout the world were invited to participate in a cluster experiment designed to explore the many possible meanings this thought-image can hold.[3]

By using the cluster process and the synthesizing abilities of the brain's right hemisphere, many people are able to discover new insights into the inner "truths" that govern their being. Many people who participated in this experiment noted that sharing creative insights into Self is one of the privileges that life can bring the aspirant.

The unexpected discoveries made in what might even seem to be a mundane, outer form are illustrated by participants who analyzed the outer form and function of a question mark. A soror writes, "Distinctive to a question mark is its purpose; it has no stops like the period, no pauses like the comma, no emphatic declarations like the exclamation point. It always contains an openness to more. It requires a response; it draws, urges, beckons something or someone else in."

Another observation on the question form is as follows, "A walking question mark is mobile, and thus can search or quest, move into obscure corners and dark places to shed light."

The shape of the question mark also elicited this comment: "The shape of the question mark looks burdened and bent, but then one thinks of the saying, 'He's not heavy, he's my brother,' and one realizes that burdens are voluntary charges. Nothing is so beautiful as the old person, stooped with his store of wisdom."

For one frater the image of the "walking question mark" took two forms that expressed to him two differences in his approach to life. "When the feet are on a path traveling in one direction there appears a man with bloated chest and inflated outer ego born of pride from his 'own' attainments. But when the feet are in the other direction there appears a man with vibrant spinal column topped with a brain that bows to the central complex of pineal and pituitary." (See Figure 27.)

Through a process of experiencing these two symbols as if they were himself, this frater came to realize that, "To be a walking question mark is to be an open-minded traveler through life. One who uses the powers of observation and discrimination to look behind the outer mask, objects and experiences. One who seeks for himself his own beingness as an integrated understanding of the individual parts of the Self which it represents. A walking question mark is a prism through which the flow of Divine Love can spread its rays upon the world, and through which the events and happenings of Life can be synthesized into one identity enabling the expression of Light in the Mind of Man."

The power inherent in this vignette is also reflected in the comments of a soror who writes, "The question mark has power: power to cleave ignorance asunder, power to lead

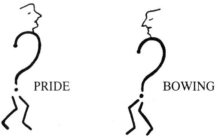

Fig. 27. *One frater's vision of the "walking question marks."*

and attract mental energy. The energy of the Mind can in turn generate knowledge."

Of the power in this symbol, another frater writes, "A question mark attitude leads to freedom. Being open to change allows me to be the person I am meaning to be." He continues, "Being open to change opens up opportunities for growth. As a result, I find that I am a happier and more integrated person. I discover within myself well-defined goals and work to do. As a walking question mark my life is interesting, more vital and productive. How can I not go forth and do what I can to create a better life for myself and those whose lives touch mine?"

Clustering as a process and technique for releasing creative power was often described by those participating in experiments and classes at Rosicrucian Park. A focus of creative power on important symbols of Self like the "walking question mark" can assist in a process of attunement with the Inner Self. Feelings and urges like "vitality, power, creative energy, openness, service, integration, freedom, enlightenment, a sense of connection with the divine in all things, a sense of purpose, boundlessness, timelessness, gratitude and acknowledgment" are among the feelings and urges people report having when they have an experience of the Inner Self. Creative expression of our inner "truths" through the process of clustering can be a doorway to an experience of the Inner Self and an aid to the mystic in his quest for self-mastery and Peace Profound.

CREATIVELY HEALING THE WHOLE PERSON

There is a tendency in our present world of good and bad, right and wrong, for many people to think that they know the only way to health and well-being. Attitudes that permit us to say, "I'm right" and, "you're wrong" have been with the human race a long time. The ancients noted that such attitudes could affect the way we perceive our world, our relationships, our visualizations of the future, our health, and our well-being. This attitude formed the basis for one of the three stages of human growth and evolution portrayed in the Mysteries of Isis in ancient Egypt and Greece, as well as the alchemical traditions of medieval times.

During the course of the year statues of Isis were draped[4] with certain colors that were also used to represent the three stages of personal growth. To the ancients, the first stage, or the color red, denoted vitality, energy, new life, child-

Fig. 28. *Image of Isis in holy garb.*

like innocence, an unconscious oneness with all of Life. This is a dream-like phase, unconscious and accepting of nature. In this stage we may feel somewhat helpless and that life should take care of us. In terms of a healing situation, the healer-patient relationship in this first phase is like a parent-child relationship.

The second stage of personal growth in the Isinian Mysteries was characterized by the colors black and white. These colors represented duality, good and bad, right and wrong, likes and dislikes. The ancients observed that such judgmental thinking led to expectations about how the world ought to be, about how we or others need to behave. In this phase we tend to focus rigidly on realities we make rather than on the actualities—the gifts Life continually creates for us.

The ancients emphasized that the phases and cycles of life were natural processes of nature. These followed each other in ordered sequence and each contributed to the unfoldment of future phases. In regard to healing this rule also applies. In the black-and-white phase, for instance, patients may begin to accept self-responsibility. Rather than expecting a parent figure to solve their problems, patients may participate by following the advice of a qualified healer, watching diet, exercise, breathing, and thinking, as well as actively visualizing and meditating. While participating in their own healing, patients may come to realize the healing potential lying within themselves.

Sometimes in the black-and-white phase the patient tries to assume total responsibility. However, this can allow us to avoid opportunities for developing healing relationships that can bring us out of ourselves. We miss opportunities to integrate with other human beings who may evoke new ways of doing things and a broader view of the world. If our visualizations, meditations, exercises, and other self-healing techniques do not appear to work, we may go further. We may deem ourselves unworthy failures. This is not self-healing. This is mental poisoning.

For the healer also, the black-and-white phase can lead to unhappiness . . . a "dark night of the soul." Regardless of healing style, whether medical or metaphysical, as healers we can have a personal need to fulfill our reality, to confirm our belief that we are good healers. When unsuccessful we may decide that we are poor healers and change our profession, or we may try to protect our belief by one or more of the following strategies:

1. *Conniving:* We will master this problem, if we just try harder, read another book, attend another lecture, take another course . . . next time it will turn out all right.

2. *Blaming:* We may decide it's the patient's fault. My therapy is fine. If only they followed my instructions, then everything would be right.

3. *Avoiding:* We may decide that this is not the kind of illness or patient we need to deal with in the future. This is not our specialty or area of expertise.

4. *Pleasing:* We can comfort ourselves and the patient by deciding that the very best is being done and that progress is being made, even if we can't see it yet.

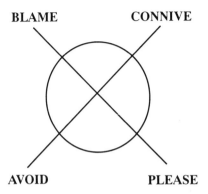

BLAME   CONNIVE

AVOID   PLEASE

Fig. 29. *Four behavioral dramas substituting for actual experience.*

Whether healer or patient, we tend to think that these four strategies help us to compete in a black-and-white world. These strategies inflate the outer personality and encourage us to think that we are in control of our lives and problems.[5] Yet, even if we are convinced of our control, if we still have the courage to go inside with an open, questioning mind, we may discover that we still secretly fear that we are not really in control, that maybe we are not really "good" healers, we only get by, we make mistakes, and we are guilty of failing.

Caught in the extremes of dualistic thinking, neither healer or patient is immune from mental poisoning. Fear, superstitious beliefs and ignorance, burn-out, despair, and degenerating health are all the legacy of dualistic thinking. The black-and-white stage represented death in the ancient mysteries; and death, in turn, putrefaction and separation in alchemy. Almost every culture of the world uses either the color black or the color white to represent death. Yet, the colors of death also symbolize the potential for rebirth and transformation to the third stage of life, represented by the color gold.

Gold is the stage of wisdom, reintegration, wholeness. The idea of a separate healer and patient loses meaning in the gold stage. In dealing with patients, we as healers gain creative insights into our own lives. Friends' needs are our needs, friends' tears our tears, friends' healing our healing. In this gold stage there is no separation between patient and healer. We are one humanity with common needs and problems, and even common transformations and healings.

Transformations occur through relationships. As the Rosicrucian studies point out, our growth and transformation does not occur by being hermits or avoiding integration with other human beings. Transmutation occurs through the tests and trials of our realities, through our interaction with others. The alchemist's work is with his realities, with what he believes to be true about the world. This subtle shift in outlook, in attitude, in consciousness, suggests that rather than our shaping life to meet our expectations, we can choose to be open to being transformed by life, and by the relationships we attract to us.

We may consciously decide to practice the art of creative healing, but this is then done without the compulsion to act out the role of healer or patient. Each time we enter into a healing relationship with others, we do not know what the precise outcome will be. We do not know in just what way our persona can be beneficially transformed. In the gold stage, entering into a healing relationship is an adventure. It is a quest that leads to ever greater self-discovery and a deeper appreciation for the love that unites all.

When a person is ill that person is vulnerable. Illness can crack our habitual defense mechanisms. When our unquestioned realities and beliefs are no longer effective, we can decide to replace them with realities that more accurately mirror our inner intentions. Upon discarding irrelevant defenses we may also be surprised to discover that we can experience greater creativity, spontaneity, and freedom.

If we are willing to let our defenses down, to look deeply within, to allow our friend to mirror our own nature, then we can come to realize the commonality, the unity, and the love that always existed but that we did not notice before. We may be surprised by our own transformations made as a result of seeing what is true in this mirror of self. We may discover at an inner psychic level there are no coincidences, that we and those attracted to us are co-healers, co-creators, on an extraordinary adventure we call life.

To embark on this extraordinary adventure, a trust in the inner power of healing and transformation is essential. Creative openness, integrity, firmness, and compassion follow from a genuine confidence or intense trust. With genuine confidence we find that no one in a relationship is less than, or more than, he or she actually is. Instead of being lost in sympathetic responses to symptoms, we interact with compassion and integrity, creatively transforming into what we actually are.

With trust, illness can be an opportunity, a threshold to greater health, to the golden state of life we call wisdom. With experience we come to realize that genuine confidence comes only when we are willing to face our own fears. Crossing this threshold results in greater physical, emotional, and mental wholeness. Rather than being the dualistic opposite of illness, health can become a celebration and appreciation of life. Life is our friend. Life is a provider of the conditions and opportunities that evoke the evolution of the open mind.

Growth, transformation, evolution can apply and be incorporated into any therapeutic modality, whether traditional or non-traditional. We can choose to follow allopathic medicine, homeopathy, chiropractic, acupuncture, touch, nutrition, or any of a host of other approaches to healing, and still realize that life is a shared adventure wherein we are all creatively evolving.

CREATIVITY AS A MARRIAGE OF THE MIND

Probably the most controversial claim made today for the processes of visualization and meditation is that they can increase creativity and native intelligence. Of course, the mystic is not simply concerned with enhanced ability to produce creative products or to raise IQ scores. Rather, the mystic is engaged in enhancing in himself a more universal perception of the world and other people, as well as promoting better choices for his activities.

Creativity and intelligence are processes, not products, and are therefore difficult to measure. But there is some evidence that visualization and meditation can enhance a person's skill in sports, business management, and daily living, and can improve a person's performance in some intellectual subjects. An experiment conducted by William Linden indicated that third graders trained in meditation were less anxious when taking tests. Certainly there is a good

CREATIVITY

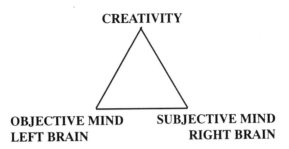

OBJECTIVE MIND   **SUBJECTIVE MIND**
LEFT BRAIN   **RIGHT BRAIN**

Fig. 30. *Contribution of each side of the brain to creative experience.*

deal of evidence from other studies that the less anxious a person is, the more effectively—within limits—he or she can think and act.

It is worth asking, though, whether relaxation is the right state for all kinds of activities. Basic research indicates that too little as well as too much arousal can lead to inferior performance. Moreover, there appears to be an optimal level of arousal for a given person during a given task. Dr. Gary E. Schwartz tested sixteen teachers of a currently popular form of meditation involving repeated intonation of a personal mantra, and a group of sixteen controls using standardized measures of creativity (the Barron-Welsh Art Scale, and a battery of tests devised by M. A. Wallace and N. Kogan). These mantra-meditators scored no better than the non-meditators. In fact, on some scales the meditators did consistently worse. This result was especially interesting because the mantra-meditators were trying hard to succeed. However, on other tests including a story-telling task used as a philosophical or projective measure of creativity, the meditators scored consistently higher than the controls.

Perhaps the explanation lies in the distinction between the functions of the left and right sides of the brain (see Figure 30). Split-brain research indicates that the two halves of the brain (the left and right cerebral hemispheres) correspond to two potentially independent "minds." The left brain hemisphere is logical, verbal, and sequential; the right hemisphere is visual, timeless, and intuitive. To the extent that visualization and meditation lead to the kind of low-arousal, and self-reflective behavior typical of right-brain activities, visualization and meditation enhance spontaneity and creativity especially in free-association tests such as storytelling. On the other hand, too much introspective, self-reflective behavior may interfere with a person's logical, left-brain activity, or the sort of problem-solving creativity required by the Wallace-Kogan Test.

What we can learn from such studies is that the germinal stages of creativity are enhanced by meditation, but if practiced to excess without concurrent development of rational thinking, it may reduce the chance of the mystic's producing and manifesting a recognizable, creative product. The distinction is important if the mystic's inner reali-

Fig. 31. *A universal symbol of thought anonymously submitted to the Master Thought Experiment. See Chapter Three. The thought expressed could also be taken as a symbol for the Marriage of the Mind.*

ties are to be actualized. The creative visualization-meditation process allows for novel integrations and for the devising of new methods and ways of doing things and reaching goals; these creative ideas often emerge from relaxed, drowsy, or twilight states of consciousness. But the expression and the validation of these ideas often requires activity, excitement, and a good deal of rational and sequential thought. Creativity in the fullest sense involves focused attention in both sides of the brain. We are indeed fortunate that these two modes of consciousness exist within each of us, and that when properly and attentively focused and harmonized, the two modes can function in a complementary and dynamic manner.

In contrast to the simple mantra form of meditation, the Rosicrucian system endeavors to recognize, value, and creatively incorporate into daily life both modes of consciousness. For this reason the ancient Rosicrucians developed concrete, step-by-step exercises for discovering and developing the powers of an integrated consciousness. The re-

Fig. 32. *An illustration, from an Indian painting, representing the "union of irreconcilables"—marriage of water and fire. The two figures each have four hands to symbolize their many different capabilities.*

sult is a "combined brain power" many times superior to the ordinary use of mind. The ancient Rosicrucian alchemists referred to this union of mind as the *mystical marriage.* Today, science has begun to explore the possibilities and values of both modes of consciousness, and new evidence is now available substantiating the old Rosicrucian knowledge that the *marriage of the mind* resolves psychological conflicts, promotes health, harmony, balance, and peace.

CHAPTER 9

CONSUMMATION OF
THE MYSTICAL MARRIAGE

Together, we have dealt with the three-fold nature of thought as experienced in a world of form. With forms we are able to come to insights. We do this by integrating our understanding of thought as (1) an object; then (2) as a technique, a process, or as a mechanism of action; and finally (3) as a symbol, model, principle, paradigm or reality—hence, dealing with thought at an objective, formative, and symbolic level of consciousness. These three states are integrated during the state of assumption, where, using active imagination we experience what it might be like if we were the force of this principle manifesting through the symbol. We find that such an integration is possible in two ways. We can either proceed from objective states of consciousness to symbolic ones, or experience symbolic states and proceed to objectify them.

In this chapter we journey to a mystical realm which lies beyond form to a realm within ourselves that transcends barriers, limits, forms, and time. We search the quintessential, inner essence at the heart of all ideas, forms, and things. This experience, then, is a transcendence to a level of vitality which lies beyond form. Any form can be enlivened by this inner essence, yet without it, outer forms are dead, lifeless, empty. If a form clothes this quintessential essence, then indeed, such a form becomes alive. Form speaks to us as art, conveying beauty and truth. The aliveness speaks to

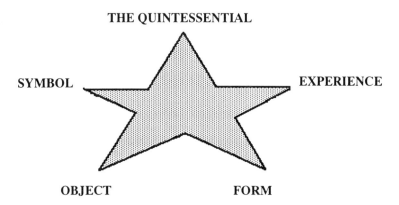

Fig. 33. *Five states of experience leading to insight, integration, and meaning.*

us and touches us. Being touched, we seek the inner beauty and truth that has touched us. We become restless and desire to experience again the touch of beauty and truth.

In ignorance, we may mistake the inner beauty and truth for the outer form. Then we are disappointed, for copies of the form are lifeless and we are not touched as we once were. Our expectations are disappointed. Also in ignorance we may demand and expect people to respond "appropriately" to the forms we employ. Again, our expectations can be disappointed. Yet, from our ignorance, our expectations and disappointments, we learn that emptiness does not touch, and aliveness cannot be feigned forever. For example, when we give a speech that touches no one, the use of platitudes does not evoke the desired result; but if we share with others that which inspires and touches us, our sensitivity, truthfulness, and vulnerability can connect us with the essence in others. Such connections evoke mutual gratitude and joy,

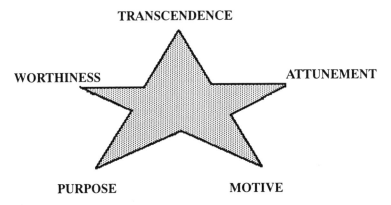

Fig. 34. *Five levels of conscious experience: objective, rational, symbolic, assumptive (active imagination), and the quintessential transcendence.*

and serve as an indication of the spiritual success of our endeavor.

The qualities of beauty and truth are actually one formless essence. Every time we connect with the soul of another person, the experience of connection is timeless, limitless, and boundless. We can be *aware* of that which is formless as we are being touched, but that which is formless is not *perceived.* Hence, we try to give a form to this essence which touches us. We try to manifest it so that we can perceive it and use it for our own purposes. There is nothing wrong in doing this. The problem comes, however, when we forget that we have clothed the vital essence in a form and we mistake what we *perceive* for *awareness* of the essence. Then, we lose awareness of the vital essence. Instead of capturing the vital essence in a form, it slips through our fingers. As the ancient Chinese mystic, Lao Tze said, "You can't capture the flow of a river in a pail, nor can you catch the wind in a bag." The flow, the Tao, the vital essence is present in every form, but cannot be captured, bound, limited in any way without our losing what it is—timeless and limitless. Put a limit on eternity and it no longer is an eternity.

Try to hold on to zest, passion, joy, peace, or any quality of our Inner Self, and it will no longer be present in our awareness. Can we be aware of eternity when we focus our perceptions on an aspect of time upon which we have set limits? Transcend these self-imposed limits of form, and we can flow in the quintessence that is life. Flowing in this quintessence, we are touched by the divinity in all forms. In this awareness, we can honor and appreciate all of nature. In this awareness, we are served by all of life. Yet, by forgetting our own true nature, we live shackled to the very forms we made for the purpose of perceiving ourselves.

We are free—but not when we think we are our perceptions. By thinking we are a body, a job, a role, a drama or facade, we will miss experiencing the genuine qualities that life is offering us. We must experience the essence of what we are and, in freedom, know the immanence of the mystical marriage. Our presence and willingness to join is lovingly awaited.

Our experience of illimitable numbers of forms, integrated by processes of insight, finally bring us to that state of silence and awe wherein we are willing to make intimate contact with the life of the soul. If we are willing to make this contact, we realize the genuine nature of love. In the metaphoric bridal chamber of the heart, we can put aside all unessentials, all technicalities, all paraphernalia of theory and speculation. We can then direct our attention into that quality at the heart of all: impersonal and illuminating love. With this focus of our attention, we are illumined with the fire of life and freed from the bondage of mental illusion and sense perception.

Our assent to the bridal chamber was marked by the destruction of old, outworn forms and the building of new forms as we reached insights with each integration of objective, rational, and symbolic form and the assumption of related spiritual principles. Now, we are to meet our soul, that vital part of us which is formless.

This new focus of attention is actually a repolarization of the consciousness, a directing of life energy inwards, inwards toward the deeper strata of being. We are ready to let go of the old focus on the purely mental or objective planes of thought and action.

There is nothing mysterious about this idea of repolarization of consciousness. A little reflection can show us how firmly held we are within the form of the personal self; the form of the mind with its opinions and views, its reasonings, and its continuous subjection to the influence and agitation of the sense life. This will be evident to us if we but recall those rare moments which come when the mind is carried beyond itself, when the mind is carried by the soul with the inspiration of creative genius. In that brief moment soul speaks to soul, and each soul recognizes its own true nature mirrored and expressed in others, and realizes its own possibilities. Consciousness is repolarized for us through our personal form being transcended. In transcendence, its range of response can be extended, can be raised

to a larger dimension. In such contact we have an intima-
tion of what we shall soon experience at will with the realization of our Mastery in Self. Thus, we realize that mind
consciousness and soul consciousness are differently experienced. Each consciousness is experienced as expressing
vastly different values and possibilities. One functions within
and is circumscribed by its self-imposed form; the other is
formless, limitless, and the source of love and inspiration.

Our work is to form temporarily a personal cosmic bridge
between the mind and soul, until the personal form is transcended and free access to the soul sphere is attained. When
the form of the bridge no longer serves a purpose, it will
pass away; for then there is a constant interplay between
mind and soul. The afflatus previously ascribed to genius
becomes a normal function of soul communion. We realize
that mind and soul are one and the stage is set within us for
our conscious realization of the marriage of "heaven" and
"earth."

In his book, *The Mystic Path,* Raymund Andrea quotes
Hugo as clearly expressing the experience of soul contact
as the soul awaits our genuine willingness to enter into a
union and partnership. Hugo writes of this repolarization
process as follows:

> Every man has within him his Patmos. He is free
> to go, or not to go, out upon that frightful promon-
> tory of thought from which one perceives the
> shadow. If he does not, he remains in the com-
> mon life, with the common conscience, with the
> common virtue, with the common faith, or with a

common doubt; and it is well. For inward peace it is evidently the best. If he goes out upon those heights, he is taken captive. The profound waves of the marvellous have appeared to him. No one views with impunity that ocean, henceforth he will be the thinker, dilated, enlarged, but floating; that is to say, the dreamer. He will partake of the poet and of the prophet. Henceforth a certain portion of him belongs to the shadow. An element of the boundless enters into his life, into his conscience, into his virtue, into his philosophy. Having a different measure from other men, he becomes extraordinary in their eyes. He has duties which they have not. He lives in a sort of diffused prayer, and, strange indeed, attaches himself to an indeterminate certainty which he calls God. He distinguishes in that twilight enough of the anterior life and enough of the ulterior life to seize these two ends of the dark thread, and with them to bind his soul to life. Who has drunk will drink, who has dreamed will dream. He will not give us that alluring abyss, that sounding of the fathomless, that indifference for the world and for this life, that entrance into the forbidden, that effort to handle the impalpable and to see the invisible; he returns to it, he leans and bends over it, he takes one step forward, then two; and thus it is that one penetrates into the impenetrable, and thus it is one finds boundless release of infinite meditation.[1]

Here then, as the frightful abyss of spirit, the oceanic sea of soul is before us, we ask ourselves if we dare to proceed into a life of change, transcendence, and uncertainty. If we dare to follow our heart, unafraid as it is, we may suddenly realize the form we are to transcend and the one we are to build, while still being fully prepared to let go of this bridging form as that release also becomes appropriate. Our choice is a simple one: to remain a prisoner within a mental and emotional form which our objective dreams have compelled us to build, or to pass beyond the frontier of a circumscribed existence into the mystic realm of the soul that is awaiting our willing approach.

Our choice in favor of the latter assumes that we accept the basic truth of mysticism: that we are not a mental being searching for a nebulous and evasive entity known as the soul, but that we are a spiritual being which is the very center of all that we are. We are, thus, the maintaining, nourishing, and energizing force vitalizing our mental, emotional, and physical life. This shift in focus from periphery to center inaugurates the realization of a spiritual essence within us, directing our everyday existence and experience. The divine, that which is boundless, limitless, and eternal, does not unite with that which is limited. That would change the essence of its nature. It unites with that within us which is also formless and unlimited. With a heart unafraid, the soul consciously merges as one with the quintessence of what is.

Is the relinquishment of the form of personality not a spiritual surrender? By no means, if the mystical marriage is to be consummated. It is that which is eternal, which cannot be lost or surrendered, and which participates in the *mysterium coniunctionis.* That which passes away is willingly released; it is not worth keeping.

The ability to discern actuality and "inner truth" is not acquired by mere wishing. Actuality, that which is, is discovered when the "inner eye" is trained to see it. In training our eyes to see, we learn to distinguish between sensation and awareness. Our physical and psychic senses, upon which we base our realities, do not reveal to us what is "true." At best, they reveal to us only the nature of forms, and even then the senses are often inaccurate.

People who identify self with their sense perceptions eventually discover that they impoverish their own lives. People who identify with their senses subordinate themselves to innate urges, annoyances, and disappointments of their bodies. A vindictive person feels no enlightenment in putting down an adversary. There is nothing immortal in embarrassment, grief, or failure. The boundless and eternal qualities of Self are to be found elsewhere.

In seeking the soul-quality of freedom, one person became ("assumed" in his inner experience) a bird. He soared and banked, climbed and dove in a boundless blue sky.

"This is freedom!" he exclaimed to himself.

"No," responded a soft voice within. "You are still perceiving."

"But if I don't perceive, how will I know that I am? I will be Nothing."

"You can choose to be aware," came the unexpected and surprising reply to his question.

Following this inner experience, the person contemplated the differences in his experiences of perceiving and simply being aware. Awareness, he discovered, was that part of his consciousness which accurately related to his surroundings. "When I am aware, there are no judgments or interpretations of what I experience, there is only the experience." Another person added, "Interpretation isn't needed. Experience just is."

When we interpret, judge, and assign value to our experiences, we make an illusory reality that can then substitute for the actual experience itself. A woman comments, "I did not have to experience those beatings, for I had my reality that they were unfair, unjust, and wrong. When I let go of my interpretations and judgments, I began to recollect an experience uncolored by my realities and perceptions."

Another person points out, "I perceive according to my reality. When my realities shift and change, I see other people and the world differently."

Many people believe their mind to be a subjective instrument. This is because they mistake their mind for their fantasies and emotional reactions, which seem to be subjective. But when our experiences have been purged of the distinctions of belief, judgment, and interpretation, then mind can achieve an objectivity. Then we can use the mind as an instrument for discerning our realities from the actuality.

To train ourselves to distinguish between illusions and the actual, we allow ourselves to experience. Experiencing without judgment and interpretation, we discover our relationship to the archetypes, the principles universally present in mineral, animal, and plant kingdoms and in all forms present in nature. We contemplate our reactions, attitudes, beliefs, and hence come to understand the advantages of following the guidance of the soul rather than blindly reacting to the events and pressures of daily life. We can contemplate purpose, meaning, significance, and the principles important to our lives, and where the opportunities lie for manifesting them. No longer need we mistake wishes, obligations, needs, fears, beliefs, and illusions for the genuine experiences of Self.

How can we remain our Self, so that we are not misled by illusions? There are a number of touchstones which can assist us in clearing illusions, and in focusing and centering in Self.

First, if something can be changed by wishing, hating, ignoring, believing, or disbelieving, *then it is not actual.* Actuality is absolute, and not a matter of whim or preference. As the poet Omar Khayyam puts it:

> The Moving Finger writes; and, having writ,
> Moves on: nor all thy Piety nor Wit
> Shall lure it back to cancel half a Line,
> Nor all thy Tears wash out a Word of it.

Our anger can often seem to be released by our venting it, yet this merely indicates that anger is not actual. By contrast, love is actual, for when love is expressed, it grows and increases. "I do not feel empty or relieved after expressing love; I feel fulfilled, connected, mysteriously whole." Such experiences of fulfillment, unity, and wholeness are hallmarks of the presence of our Inner Self and the touch of actuality.

As another person adds, "When I am sad or disappointed, a good cry helps me in overcoming the disappointment," because again, for all its poignancies and pain, disappointment is not actual. If it were actual, then it could never be washed out by tears.

Neither will beliefs prevail. If we have become disappointed by our marriage, for example, we may try to create the illusion that our spouse is unromantic, dull, and the cause of great misery. Yet, changing this belief will change only our attitude. The belief was not actual. Substituting one belief for another belief may help us appear more enlightened, but will not necessarily help us get in touch with actuality. Irresponsibility is not an archetypal force of life.

The beloved sister of one man committed suicide while his wife spoke with her on the telephone and he was rushing to his sister's side. The sister was dead on his arrival. For years grief gripped him and his wife. Yet, this grief and pain was not actual either. Actuality lay in the timeless, indestructible connection the three of them shared. Death, alcoholism, drug abuse, or any passing thing or behavior cannot shatter what is actual. The actuality of our soul abides even in the midst of turmoil and strife.

A second hallmark is that if what we are perceiving can be known by our physical senses, then it is not actual. For example, we do not discern actuality by merely listening to a Beethoven Symphony, but rather by appreciating its beauty and harmony.

A third touchstone is to realize that actuality resides in the essence of that which we call *God*. As we experience any aspect of life, we can choose to attune with these divine qualities. With this touchstone we can discern if we are attuning with the actual within every circumstance of life, or whether we are choosing to focus elsewhere.

Discernment involves more than just being able to discriminate between the actual and the outer form. We can learn to *invoke* the archetypal forces of the actual. This is an integral part of living, training the mind to bring the awareness of "heaven" to our perceptions of "earth." With this conscious knowledge and activity, we become a chalice in which the conjunction of this heaven and earth can take place.

The invocation of "inner truth" is the central theme of a Quest for the Holy Grail. The treasure in this adventure is the right to be a bearer and protector of the Chalice of Light. The right is earned by demonstrating our responsibility, our competence, and our love for what is genuine and actual.

In our lives, actuality is invoked in five ways: As we engage in the activities of our lives, we invoke the actual by searching for the meaningful and purposive in what we do. If our purpose in living is only to make money and achieve personal fame, we are not dwelling in actuality, for those are passing illusions of an egocentric selfishness. On the other hand, if our purpose is to serve others and civilization instead of self, then we may indeed find meaningfulness in what we do, for those purposes are linked to Light—that is, with divine archetypes.

As we interact with other people, we discern actuality by experiencing and sharing qualities that also touch and inspire them. In other words, we willingly experience inspiration, allowing our love, forgiveness, endurance, hope, and patience to be quickened within ourselves. Then, we share these meaningful qualities with others so that actuality can be a mutual realization. Together we attain an understanding of our divine origin.

As we live our daily lives, we invoke actuality by touching our immortality. Immortality is touched at the level of our Inner Self which is timeless and deathless—which cannot be lost and therefore never has to be found or saved. Experiencing the Inner Self, we transcend all that the body does, the emotions feel, the mind thinks. Together, we discover that immortality, perfection, and wholeness exist now —in actuality, in the highest portions of our being. As we integrate this realization into the personality, the wholeness within us mingles with the seeds of our character in every phase of our lives, assisting us in realizing the inner perfection present in all things and circumstances.

Most importantly, the invocation of actuality is characterized by a *love of truth*. Clear vision can be attained when there is a dedication to integrity. The shackles of illusion can be snapped when there is a deep awe and reverence for the majesty and splendor of the universe. Truth can be revealed when love burns in the heart. If we but love God with all our soul, heart, and mind, then divinity is discerned in the midst of the myriad forms of creation. Our reverence for the divinity within all of life opens our eyes and we see life. Our love of truth draws truth to us, lifts us up, and even in the midst of form, we come to dwell in a higher realm.

As an "agent of omneity," aware of and appreciating the Light in all things and in all circumstances, acknowledging and sharing joy, living in profound gratitude as a gift of living, we suddenly realize that the conjunction of heaven and earth, sun and moon, light and form, left brain and right brain, are all finding unity and expression through us. In love with truth, we experience truth, and we become the bearer of truth and inspiration for an awaiting humanity. In this profound moment we may come to know the meaning of our own participation in the mystical marriage, the marriage of the mind, and the conjunction of heaven and earth.

Down through countless eons of time we have searched for truth and beauty in an outer world of form. Beauty, Truth patiently awaited us within the bridal chamber of our own heart. In love we are joined, in the active expression of our joined efforts we are consummated, and in our sharing, seeds are planted and the divine child is born anew. In a world of form and egocentric strife, we learn mastership in Self, we learn love, and we come to know joining.

CHAPTER 10

THE MASTERS AMONG US

A t the heart of each person there is a radiant light that has the power to manifest the heart's most fervent desires. If we are all in possession of such radiant power, why do we not fully enjoy life? Why do we not possess in full measure all the love, all the peace, all the inner treasures that have always been the promise of humanity since the most ancient of days?

We all want love, compassion, sensitivity, and trust. We want these qualities from other people. We also want others to believe that we give love, sensitivity, compassion, and trust to them. Yet, most of the time we feel there are barriers that stand in the way of our receiving or giving such love to other people. What could possibly stand in the way of our sharing the Light, Life, and Love that is the essence of each one of us?

I have often experienced the honor and privilege of being with people in the sacred temples of the Rosicrucian Order, AMORC. These temples are made sacred by the thought and conduct of those participating. Rather than choosing to come to a Rosicrucian Temple, these people could have chosen to stay home watching television, reading a book, or doing any of the things we do on weekday evenings to entertain and occupy ourselves; but instead, these people chose to attend a Rosicrucian Temple. Those of us present in the Temple chose to be there with one another, to share the sacred Light with which we are entrusted. To be there with such people is indeed a privilege and honor.

Mystics, adepts, masters have all spoken and written about processes for letting go the barriers to sharing this Light with each other. In various centuries, these mystics have written that this Light was present in the very first, primordial matter. They have written that all that has been created was created through the agency of this Light. This is the same Light that is the Light of Eternal Man. It has been written that it is this Light that shines in our darkness, but that this darkness cannot master it or even hold it back. Such words can give us hope, the hope that we too can let down our barriers to the Light, that we too can acquire Mastery in Self, and that we too can radiate unimpeded the Light that we are.

As children, we thought that we could be hurt and that we could be injured. We thought that we would experience pain. To protect ourselves from pain we erected walls, walls of protection, walls that would make us safe, walls that would allow us to look right and be good in the eyes of other people. But, what these walls now do is hide the Light from others and hide the Light from ourselves. The truth is that the Light of the Inner Self cannot be diminished or enhanced, or injured in any way. We did not realize this when we erected barriers. We did not realize this when we thought the walls of protection made us beautiful and made us special. We did not realize this when we thought that, without these defenses, we would be nothing. We would be vulnerable. We would be alone. If we were alone, then we might as well give up.

Walls of protection cast their own shadows. Since we perceive the world in our own minds, we perceive it in the shadows and darkness cast by our own walls of protection. Such dark perceptions give us good reason to fear, good reason not to trust either life or other people. Yet, these fears and the lack of trust are merely due to shadows, shadows cast by walls of our own making.

There are four different walls of protection which we erect (see Figure 35). They appear whenever our perceptions are based on Fear. We experience these four barriers as confining us, locking us up within the walls of a very personal prison. When we move to get out of this prison, our perception is distorted and we feel like we are going deeper and deeper into this personal prison. We can fear that we will never be able to experience genuine freedom.

The first barrier consists of a *Wall of Impossibility*. Behind this barrier of impossibility we believe that "I can't." "I can't do this. I can't do what I want to do. I can't." When we experience the impossibilities of this world, we experience despair. Despair tempts us to quit all together, to quit trying because there seems no way to accomplish anything. We think and feel we are weak and powerless. This feeling brings us to the existential question of Hamlet, "To be or not to be." We question whether it is better to live or die. We question our basic self-worth. We deny life and our Inner Self as the sole carrier of our worth. Hence, it is here, against the Wall of Impossibility that we are given the ultimate choice of Life or Death. It is here we come to discover the answer to our questions, "What is worthiness? What must we do to be worthy? Is life worth living without the power to make the world be the way we think it needs,

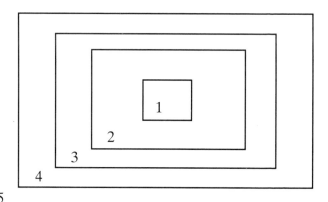

Barrier	What We Say	What We Experience
1. Impossibility	I can't	Despair
2. Survival	I need	Desperation
3. Obligation	I must	Guilt, Anger
	Should	Bitterness
	Have to	You owe me
	Ought	Dissatisfaction
4. Desire	I want	Longing, disquiet, disease

.... I Choose..

5. Freedom	I am willing	Inner self qualities
6. Freedom	I am grateful	Entheos
7. Freedom	I am enjoying	Cosmic Consciousness

Fig. 35. *Becoming Free.*

should, and we desire it to be? Do I have the strength and vitality to continue in such a world as this?"

If we manage to let go of this Wall of Impossibility, let go of our beliefs, thoughts, and feelings of "I can't," we come to the second barrier, the *Wall of Survival.* Here we confuse our self-identity with our instrument, the body. We say, "I need." We believe that, as a body, we need: we need to eat, we need to drink, we need to sleep. These are fundamental needs of a self-image controlled by a body. When we fear that our needs are not going to be met, we experience desperation. When we need anything at all, the need is desperate and we experience fear. The fear denies the possibility that we may be more than just a body. With incredible courage the Rosicrucian student may choose to face this fear and ask of self, "Am I just a body? What am I actually?"

If we go through this Wall of Survival, we come to a third barrier, the *Wall of Obligation.* Here we say, "We must. I must, I should, I ought, I have to, I got to." Here, against this Wall of Must, Shoulds, and Oughts of obligations to man-made rules and laws, we experience guilt, resentment, regret. We feel that the world owes us and we will "see to it that others feel guilty" too if they don't do as we expect. Here, against the Wall of Obligation, the student may come to ask, "Am I not more than limits and demands? Am I only a thing to be used? Am I not something more than this?"

As we get through this Wall of Obligation we come to the fourth barrier, the *Wall of Desire.* Here we find that, "I want." This is the most subtle of the four walls. After all, we live in a society that tells us we should want a car, we should want to be successful, we should want to have a house. Yet, when we want, we make our inner happiness dependent on the outside world. Rather than joy, we experience longing, disquiet, disease. If we can see that we have *choice,* that we choose the direction our life takes, that we are responsible for the results of our choices, that we have power to make new choices and give new directions—that gets us through this fourth wall. Here we can discover that we have the power to choose from deep within our hearts what it is we are to do in life. Choosing even small things can be important to the discovery of this inner power and strength, like choosing to breath, eat, and sleep. Then, suddenly we are free of all four barriers.

Outside the walls we experience *Freedom.* The first level of Freedom is "I am willing." Here we experience the gifts of our Inner Self. In our laboratories, people report that when they are experiencing the Inner Self they report experiencing "love," "peace," "oneness," "unity," "wholeness," "compassion," "trust," "confidence," "timelessness," "the absence of barriers," "complete freedom." All these gifts are expressed when we are willing to experience life, rather than make our life experience wrong. When we are willing, we find that we can let go of saying we "should" and "ought" and that others also "should" and "ought." Rather than saying this is what we "should have experienced," we are willing to experience what life brings us. Rather than interpreting the way it "ought" to be (after all, "we know best") we are willing to experience the gifts of life just as they are.

When we can say, "I am willing" we can go to the next level of freedom, "I am grateful." Here we experience the *Entheos,* a Greek word made up of *en,* meaning "within," and *theos*, meaning "God," which together means "God within." We get the word *enthusiasm* from this magical word meaning "God within." Dr. H. Spencer Lewis spoke of this level of consciousness where we are grateful. He suggested that when we pray we don't have to just ask for things of desire; rather we can choose to express the gratitude that already is in our heart. Our gratitude can open us to experience the Law of Attraction.

When we are grateful, we may also experience the third level of freedom. We experience "I am enjoying, I am joyful in every circumstance." We can feel and express joy in every experience, every circumstance of life. A tall order! A tall order, to experience joy in all circumstances. What about the circumstances we say are wrong, unfair, and unjust? Are we willing to experience joy and feel gratitude when we make such judgments? When we are willing, we attune to the boundlessness and limitlessness of Self. Such an experience of boundlessness in the Cosmic is what we call *Cosmic Consciousness*.

Mystics, adepts, masters have each been willing to let down barriers and to express the Light, Life, and Love that is within the heart of every human being. How difficult it can seem at times to see this, and yet it's always there for us when we are willing, grateful, and cheerful.

Rosicrucians, mystics, and adepts have written about serving as examples of what it is to express the Light, Life, Love that is within our hearts. As ideals, these mystics, adepts, and masters each serve as a source of inspiration, a source of guidance, a source of assistance—all because they are willing that essence which we all are. Hence, in sharing our willingness, gratitude, and joy, each one of us is able to demonstrate that "the master resides within the temple." "It is the God within that dwells within the temple, who dwells in the human heart and finds power in the human brain." With this inner voice of power, "the agents of evil tremble in the abyss, the four elements prove willing to serve us and the highest intelligences are ambitious to obey our innermost desires."

This is not the blind following of external masters. This is not a compulsive fatalism, or the obedience to external gurus, worldly masters, or tyrants that would have us follow them as if we were puppets dancing on the strings of fear, impossibility, need, obligation, or desire. These are merely the strings of fear and belief. They do not have the power to compel our action and thereby restrict our freedom. The power to choose action and freedom abides within ourselves.

As students of mysticism, are we willing to let go of shadows and echoes that resound through our minds and keep from us the truth of who we actually are? Are we willing to let go and let fears and shadows fade from our consciousness, being ever aware that darkness is merely the absence of Light? If we are willing to let go and we are willing to abide with the inner master, the Inner Self, if we are willing to abide with the radiant energy of who we actually are, then it is that all the gifts are there for us to share with all those we love. Then, also, we can realize that we are not alone, that the Great Work that we undertake has been undertaken by mystics, adepts, and masters, Rosicrucians, Martinists, and others who have abided among us throughout the ages. They form a great chain of being, a chain of being wherein each heart has expressed a willingness to let go the barriers, a gratitude for life the way it is, a joy in sharing this life in love with each other. This is a powerful chain, a chain of which we are a part and hold a rightful place.

When we are willing to let go the barriers of fear, belief, resentment, regret, guilt; when we are willing to pass through the walls of I can't, I need, I must, and I want; we can then realize that we are not alone, that a Light leads the way as it does in every heart that has expressed its willingness, its gratitude, and its joy. We can know that in Rosicrucian Temples, Lodges, Chapters, and Pronaoi and in our Home Sanctums, there are lights on our Shekinah or altar to commemorate the Greater Light within each one of us. Within this Light we can abide in stillness and reverence, that we may allow all shadows to pass from our consciousness, being ever aware that darkness is merely the absence of Light. In Peace Profound, let us remember who we actually are.

Shadows of shadows of the shadow of His face;
Echoes of echoes of the echoes of His word.
The shadows pass, the substance remains.
Multitudes of tomorrows melt into yesterday
Save one that will dawn as today without end,
Has already dawned and risen is its sun
For him who is awake, whose heart is a full moon,
Holy witness of the wealth it reflects.

It beams forth what it sees, bright into our darkness,
For us moonlight, but for the moon, daylight
From a fountain in flood ever-flowing.

Truth, All-Knowing, Eternal Lord
Of the Absolute Day beyond day and night,
Infinite Beatitude, as we meet together, answer us,
    guide us
Over the surge of this sea of shadows, this vast
Ocean of echoes, that on the ultimate shore
We may behold and hear, and have and be.

God of our Hearts, God of our Realization,
Thou hast given us the Rose and the Cross
That we who are raised in the Order
May know the truth, in Love, in Art, and in Science.
How manifold are Thy works!
Bestow Thy blessing upon our presence here
That we who are raised in Order
May discern Truth and know the Beauty in All.

George F. Buletza

CHAPTER 11

FREEDOM

E xploring qualities of inner experience has been one of the endeavors of the Rosicrucian research facilities. In 1986 and 1987 Dr. David Aguilera joined me in this exploration into transcendence, insight, and the experience of Self. Willingness, gratitude, and joy are among the qualities that we explored together. What follows are explorations of these three Levels of Freedom introduced in Chapter 10.

THE WILLINGNESS TO BE OURSELVES

Life in this world often seems tumultuous and full of strife. In this kind of world we may feel that defensiveness, conflict, isolation, anger, defeat, anxiety, confusion, and being victimized are all attributes of "living." Yet, is this living? Is there not another way? What does it take to Live, to express the Light of our Inner Self? What attitudes allow us to share ourselves with each other?

Some people describe being our Inner Self as a child-like way of returning to Life. Some subjects describe this child-like state as "simple," "clear," "relaxed," "being myself," "discovering who I am," "innocent," "risky," "exciting," "adventurous," "joy," as "a willingness to experience."

Some people find that joy is forgotten or denied in fearful circumstances. Yet, these circumstances are an opportunity to renew our willingness. As one person points out,

"As much as I find experiences of Self to be joyful and fulfilling, I also find that I need to come back to my own ways and attitudes that ensure my success. This is safe, being child-like is not." To choose willingness when we "know" it's not safe takes courage and perseverance.

Becoming our Self takes courage. Becoming our Self means letting go of outer aspects of personality. "I find that when I'm successfully into my facade, I think I'm looking good in others' eyes. That feels 'good' to me. But unfortunately, I also feel guilty and scared that I might be found out. Then, I feel even more defensive." Another agrees. "When I'm not being who I actually am . . . I feel that I'm a failure. What's ridiculous is that I'm much more powerful in just being who I am." "When I forget, my fears are realized."

"When I represent myself as superior, I'm still well aware that it's a facade." Yet, this facade can seem very important to us. "I cling to my facades and worry over what could happen if I expose myself." "I'm afraid that I'll appear simple, dumb, stupid." Based on fear of exposure we build within ourselves a *need* to maintain a false front. "My front protects me when I fear trusting others or myself. For me it is an issue of trust."

Facades appear in many forms. "I need to be in control." "Being right is important to me." "It's worth anything to be right." "I don't want other people to see my weaknesses." "I don't want people to see what I can't see. When they show me what I'm doing, I'm humiliated."

"I feel I am myself when I'm fulfilling my obligations. Of course, even when I'm doing my duty, it's still not enough." "It's never enough." "No one appreciates how much I do." "I can't ever rely on others to do things right." "Why am I always so tired and unappreciated?"

There are others who feel just the opposite. "I'm myself whenever I've no responsibilities. I'm me when I'm free." "Why do people always want to put restrictions on me, make me follow stupid rules, make me do things I don't want to? You can't be yourself if you're not free to experience life." "Pretending that I'm free when I know I'm not, is not real."

Each of us can build individual defenses which allow us to feel safe, but also separate and alone. Each protection is based on an anxiety, worry, or fear. "When I feel unsure, or worse, challenged in my beliefs, I angrily defend myself. Afterwards, I feel guilty and wish I had given myself time to adjust to new beliefs and realities."

When we experience an unexpected flush of feeling we may fend off the feeling and become rigid in our behavior. "When I'm afraid, I become too formal and don't allow myself to experience the moment. Later, I often wish I had, because the new experience was just what I had been looking for." Fearing to be exposed and vulnerable, we can choose to keep up our guard, missing opportunities to share and experience ourselves.

If we choose to let go of fear and defensive beliefs, we are then free to be our Inner Self. "Before I let go of a defensive belief, I can fear that I'm going to suffer a small death, that I'll look ridiculous, that I might actually be grateful and then I'll be humiliated for my previous attitude. Afterwards, however, what I actually feel is joy, freedom, and even a physical lightness. I am grateful once again to let go of my fear and reality." "I am grateful . . . for I am not a victim! I feel my inner power returned." " . . . I feel my personal power." " . . . I feel my genuine power."

"When I let go of my old belief, I consciously tell myself that I have finished with my old way of relating to people. I make a choice based on willingness to change my reality. Each time I choose, my willingness empowers me. My willingness makes possible and even commands a change to occur." This is Mastery. This mastery is a process which is personal to each of us and which is based on a willingness to change. As one person put it, "I am finally realizing what I really am."

In our "change" process, we walk through a threshold, finding on the other side that keeping our facade is of no value. Unconsciously, we may have felt that either being "right," or looking good, fulfilling obligations or avoiding them was protective, but now find that our inner "truth" is the only genuine security. "As long as I stay with my conscience, I am standing on truth. I am no longer vulnerable to the shifting sands of the world and popular opinion." "When I experience my Inner Self, the world is joyful and golden. I no longer am caught in what appears to be strife and tumult." "I thought mastery was being in control. Yet, it is the free-flowing, open sharing of myself that brings joy and a rapport with others." "In my fear of exposing weakness, I'm guarded in revealing myself to others. Yet, in sharing myself, I'm finding the kind of trust and love I've always wanted."

By coming to experiences of the Inner Self, we discover a hope and a confidence that can reawaken our consciousness when we again forget and cling to protective facades. We are inspired to ask, "What does it take to share the Light of our Inner Self?" "Willingness" and "Trust" are two frequent responses.

With these two responses we now know, in both the world and in our hearts, that there is another way, a way that offers joy, freedom, love, and all the treasures sought in life's adventure.

The following questions are for our personal self-examination, contemplation, and our own exploration of our willingness.

1. Am I willing to experience myself in all circumstances? Am I willing to experience joy and sadness, confidence and anxiety, fulfillment and failure, innocence and confusion, peace and conflict, trust and defensiveness, connection and separation, acceptance and rejection, and so on?

2. Am I willing to experience Self, or is it more important to look good and be right? In my life, which am I choosing? Let us take a moment to experience our choice.

3. I experience courage, openness, inner guidance when I . . . and I experience fear, separation, guilt, and impossibility when I . . . .

4. I want to experience new realities in the following areas of my life: Am I willing to experience these new attitudes even if I were to look ridiculous?

5. I am genuinely willing to acknowledge who I am in the following areas: . . . I am not willing to change my realities (i.e., beliefs, interpretations, expectations, judgments) in these other areas: . . . .

6. Am I willing to experience free-flowing, open sharing of myself, joy, trust, rapport with others, love, and am I also willing to experience rigidity, protection, sadness, loneliness, and fear? Am I willing to experience all that life, the Cosmic, offers me?

7. Being already Light, let us picture a sea of blackness. Let us breathe deeply into our inner picture, intensifying and giving life to our experience. What is on the other side of this dark sea? In every moment of my life, which am I choosing?

8. What does it take for me to share the Light that I am?

GRATITUDE

Dr. H. Spencer Lewis frequently spoke of that level of experience where we are grateful. He suggested that when we pray we should not just ask for things of desire; rather we can choose to express the gratitude that is already in our hearts. Is there a mysterious power in our experience of gratitude? Can we attain such power in our own lives? What could possibly hold us back?

Gratitude is a quality of our experience that is thought by some to be a virtue and by others to be a weakness. Depending on our realities and desires we may look at gratitude as either natural or foolish. We may ask, "Can we be grateful when we are feeling despair, when we don't have what we think we need, what is just, or what we want?"

For instance, one person experienced sexual abuse as a child. Her response to life is anger and attack. Her experience in life is separation and loneliness, which is also her subconscious fear. Letting go of her aggressive protections is still difficult. "I'd like to escape, but there's nothing I can do. It is scary. That's the way I always feel, though. I escape from everything I feel. I make excuses. I just don't want to have this experience. I rebel!"

Like this person, some people point out, "When I feel despair, life is impossible. This is the way life is and I can't change it, then I don't feel grateful." "It's impossible to feel gratitude when I know life's unjust." "I know it. It's unfair, it's unjust. You want me to feel grateful for this?"

"Life doesn't give me what I need. I've got to work for it, strive and fight for it." "I've earned everything I've got. No one gives me anything I need." "Gratitude isn't something I often feel except on Sunday or maybe Thanksgiving." "I can give you gratitude when I've earned it for myself." Yet, another points out, "When I feel I've earned what I got, that sucks the gratitude right out of it."

"Of course, I feel grateful when I get what I want. Only why can't I get what I want when I want it?" "If I haven't got what I want by Tuesday you can't expect me to feel gratitude on Wednesday." "You wonder why I'm irritable?"

Mystics can discover that we ask for the experiences we receive, even to the choice of our own parents. One member recalled for us some prenatal and childhood experiences:

> I can remember seeing myself as a round, glowing sphere. Yet, I knew that the sphere itself was not me, but merely an expression of my being. In front of me, I could see two women. I knew that they were sisters, that the one I chose was to be my mother and the other to be my aunt. One of them held the attraction of love and nurturance which would have shielded and encompassed me throughout my childhood. With the other the attraction was a deep sense of responsibility. I chose wisely, relinquishing this opportunity for an all-encompassing, fulfilling love. I chose for my mother the woman who represented responsibility. As I grew up, however, my biological mother became less involved in parenting, and my aunt— my psychological mother, took over the parenting role. As for my father, he was a very difficult man. He was physically, mentally, and emotionally abusive.
>
> It was not until later in life, during an initiation ritual in the Atrium degrees, that I truly realized the significance of my childhood experiences. During the initiation, I had a profound sense of attunement with my Inner Self, at which moment I

felt prompted to ask some question which had been burning in my heart. I chose to ask, "Why is the relationship with my father so very difficult?" The answer shot back, "Because you are so much like him." This response was gradually accepted by my outer consciousness, and over the years I have come to realize the shadow side of my personality.

I now feel truly grateful for both of my parents. Had I been raised by my aunt in a totally loving, engulfing environment, I would never have let loose of her apron strings, satisfied instead to be encompassed by her love. I would not have been desirous of entering the world at large. I am grateful for my father because through him I came to know myself. Suffering now is irrelevant. I can now experience gratitude and can now realize that I have received what I asked for.

"When I recognize that I am realizing qualities of Self I have asked for, then I can't help but experience gratitude." "Often I don't feel gratitude at first because my experience doesn't fit my picture of what I think I should be grateful for. If my expectations are not met, I don't feel grateful, but later may realize that I have received what I hoped for." "I hope to experience what I can be grateful for. But hope is often colored by expectations that stand in the way of gratitude." "The experience of gratitude is followed by such joy that I only wish that I could always be open to that."

People who experience genuine gratitude find that it is spontaneous, natural, and free. "Gratitude is often unexpected. It's just here." "Gratitude is always here, even though I can't always feel it." "The more I'm willing to accept gratitude as a part of life the more intense it becomes. Then it becomes more and more natural." "I can't make it happen. I can be open to it. When gratitude is here it's a gift." "When I am grateful I feel light, joyful, connected." " . . . I feel centered, harmonious, peaceful." " . . . I feel positive toward the world, genuinely tuned into things, positive towards others."

"Intuitively, I know it's possible to experience gratitude in all circumstances. Getting there is the difficulty." "I'm not willing to experience gratitude if I don't have my way." "I can experience gratitude in all circumstances where I'm willing to experience life as it is. This means I need to let go of thinking I know how it should be."

The willingness to open to experiences of gratitude can take courage. One Rosicrucian student describes her experience as follows:

I wanted to let go of the negative emotions I experienced whenever I thought of childhood beatings. I asked my Inner Self for assistance. When I started to let go, my ego went crazy. It said to me, "How could you possibly do this. Everyone would agree these beatings were terrible and wrong. If you do this everyone will know you are crazy."

My inner self merely replied, "Do you want to let go or not?"

My ego replied, "You've already forgiven your father. You don't need to do this." Indeed, I thought I had forgiven my father.

My inner self merely asked, "Do you want to let go or not?"

I replied, "Yes," and I asked my inner self, "What was my interpretation that is still generating my negative emotions?"

My inner self responded, "The beatings were unfair, unjust, and wrong!"

The ego exclaimed, "If you do this, you are going to feel gratitude for those beatings, then everyone will know for sure that you're crazy!"

The inner self responded with the same question, "Do you want to let go or not?"

"Yes, I choose to let go of unfair, unjust, and wrong." This was scary.

I then experienced those beatings, possibly for the first time. Letting go of the interpretation, I indeed experienced gratitude. I interpreted this to mean that "never again would I need to fear being beaten up by life."

The Tom-tom Legend of the American Plains Indians teaches that to become a Peaceful Warrior, the brave must be happy, see the Great Spirit in all things, and give thanks in every situation. Half a world away, Paul wrote to the Thessalonians, that to become true Christians they should, "Rejoice always, pray constantly, give thanks in all circumstances . . . . "

People attest to the genuine power and freedom experienced with gratitude. Dr. Lewis and our subjects demonstrate that for us gratitude is already burning in each of our hearts. Hence, the choice we face is between joy and fear. Are we willing to experience gratitude and joy or will we choose to remain with fear and judgment? The Peaceful Warrior and the Rosicrucian Knight vanquish fear with a courageous thrust of gratitude.

The following questions are for our personal self-examination, contemplation, and our own exploration of our willingness.

1. Is there a genuine willingness in my heart to experience gratitude?

2. Do I have the courage to experience gratitude even when others may make me wrong?

3. Am I willing, grateful, and happy or is it more important that I believe that I am right, look good, that I am safe?

4. At this moment am I experiencing inner strength, inner trust, inner confidence, inner connection, inner peace, and gratitude or do I feel separate, do I need to escape from experience, do I feel life is impossible, do

I feel despair, desperation, guilt, desire for life to be different from the way it is at this moment?

5. Choose a major life problem or issue. In this matter, what would it take me to trust my inner guidance?

6. In this matter what is right, just, and correct? Am I willing to let go of this?

7. Am I willing to accept all my experiences, all aspects of what I really am? Am I willing to accept what I am experiencing right now?

8. In this moment now, am I willing to wait with bated breath for the return of willingness, gratitude, and joy?

IN SEARCH OF THE MYSTIC'S JOY

"Joy is the most infallible sign of the presence of God," wrote Teilhard de Chardin. In contemplating his own experience of joy, C. S. Lewis expressed the idea that joy is that quality of our experience that when it seems to go away, we simply wait with bated breath for its return. These comments indicate that the experience of joy is a noetic/aesthetic gift that simply comes and goes, and then returns without our control. Without a sense of personal control, does this mean that our desire for joy is hopeless, or is there a conscious attitude that welcomes an experience of joy? Is this spiritual experience the very essence of what is sought by the mystic?

In experiencing the mystical, one subject commented, "There is a quality within me that when I touch it, my mind expands and I experience the fullness of the Cosmic. While in this expansive state, I experience no desires, no obligations, no needs, and no impossibilities. The mundane melts away and I know peace, wholeness, and, most wonderfully, joy."

This subject's comment agrees with the perspective suggested by the eminent Swiss psychiatrist, Carl Jung. In speaking about happiness, he states:

> Since it is a subjective state whose reality cannot be vouched for by any external criterion, any further attempt to describe and explain it is doomed to failure, for only those who have had this experience are in a position to understand and attest its reality. "Happiness," for example, is such a remarkable reality that there is nobody who does not long for it, and yet there is not a single objective criterion which would prove beyond all doubt that this condition necessarily exists. As so often with the most important things we have to make do with the subjective judgment.[1]

If the experience of joy is indeed a subjective state, then what attitudes will allow joy to flower? "Joy is a being function. You don't make being do anything. Being just is." Another person adds, "Joy is a pleasurable emotion requiring my willingness to be open to it. I can give permission for my experiencing joy, but I don't force it to happen."

Joy can be such an important virtue that we may try to insist that it always be present. However, as one subject points out, "Willing joy doesn't work for me. Joy is a gift that appears spontaneously, transcending my ordinary self." Some subjects point out that an egocentric willing can be transmuted to a spiritual openness. "I feel joy when I am interested and focused to such an extent that I forget myself. Then I am enthusiastic and spontaneous. The joy I experience is spontaneous."

Many people at this point ask, "Why do some people have more joy than others? Why do some people get more gifts?" In asking these questions are we more involved in ourselves or in others, or in our experience? By not forcing joy, by being involved in experience, self is forgotten and subjects suggested that joy simply follows.

In asking some subjects what might happen if they were open to experiencing joy, some subjects discussed attitudes blocking their experience of joy. Subjects were asked, "If I were joyful, then . . . ." They responded, "I won't be accepted," "I'll be out of control," "I won't be real. I'll be crazy," "They'll think I'm crazy."

"They will think I'm one of those overzealous religious fanatics!" "I won't be grounded. I'll be up in the clouds somewhere and won't be able to relate to others. I'll be rejected." "My friends will think I'm weird. They will think something is wrong with me. They may prefer to see me as mad. After all, they may prefer such a judgment rather than accepting the responsibility and possibility that they too could be joyful."

Besides concern about the opinions of others, one person indicated a more basic fear: "Darkness hates the light.

It would be better to hide out. You've got to be careful about showing your light."

Some people admitted to subconscious fears in responding to the question, "If I were to have fun like this, then . . . ." "I wouldn't get any work done," "I'd be fired," "My God! I wouldn't be taken seriously!" "It's the best way of ending up on a cross that I know of."

Being joyful can also mean letting go of facades. "I wouldn't be able to be unhappy or a martyr," "I wouldn't be able to participate in that sad game at the funeral," "They might say your being disrespectful for the dead."

We may avoid dealing with our personal fears. Yet, what does it cost us in terms of joy to avoid dealing with fear? Subjects responded, "Just about the whole shooting match." "It cuts the heart out of my experience of life. The meaning is gone." "I don't have near enough fun now that I'm all grown up." "It costs me my happiness. It's doom and gloom." "Joy? What's that?"

For many there is a cost in terms of health: "You die, a little, but at once." "You are cutting yourself off from the Source, the Source of vitality." "Joy is my Fountain of Youth. Without it I feel prematurely old, lifeless."

Others speak of cost in terms of relationships: "It makes my relationships disconnected, disjointed. There is a sense of isolation. You are in your own little world, the one you've created." "The world seems colorless, gray, dark, dreary."

Costs are often obvious, but the payoffs can be more difficult to identify. In asking the question, "What are the payoffs we get from believing that joy is not permissible?" subjects replied, "You get to feel sorry for yourself." "I'm not responsible for my misery." "I have no choice."

By telling ourselves we have no control in our lives, we can rationalize our misery, our moods and attitudes. "Those are the breaks." "My misery is all right." "I get to be right that there is no joy here for me." "I get to be as selfish as I want." "You get to put up with a lot of miserable people who also put up with my bellyaching."

For many people projecting their fear onto others can be another payoff. "You can shift blame." "God did it to me. It's all his fault." "Since I'm not happy there is no good reason for anyone else to be. It's all right that I judge others for their inappropriate feelings."

Without joy, life can seem so desperate that even a facade of joy can seem preferable to a seemingly empty life. Yet, many people point out that there's a difference between joy as an experience and joy as a facade in order to look good and seem alive. "When I think I'm supposed to be joyful, joy is no longer genuine. I simply play a role." "It's like I know what it's supposed to look like, so I play it. It's a drama. Its not genuine." "I put a funny grin on my face to indicate that everything's okay, that I'm joyful. But this kind of drama is not who I am."

Joy is more than a facade, drama, or role. Many subjects indicated that there is a particular attitude present when genuine joy is experienced. "If I'm going to be joyful, it starts with the willingness to experience." An interpretation of our experience is not the same as the willingness to experience. "It's the willingness to experience—period. It includes sadness, the full range of my emotions. My experience of joy stops when I interpret, when I make my experience wrong or bad." Any judgment, even the interpretation of ourselves being right, good and ideal, can inhibit the experience of joy. "When I am self-righteous I don't have to fear being wrong; I feel self-justified, but also isolated and alone, and there is no joy in that."

"To be joyful, willingness is the key. Then it happens, it all falls into place. That's the magic." "The secret here for me is my willingness to experience gratitude. When I experience gratitude, joy often follows." Here, gratitude means that shared feeling which brings people even closer together, not the polite "thank you" which follows as a payoff for a service rendered. "When I am profoundly grateful, I feel a sense of connection with others, or even with the cosmic whole. My being fills with a light and love which transcends feeble words." "The same spiritual essence is present in gratitude as is present in joy. They are connected. It's as though gratitude and joy are two means to arrive at the same experience of self."

Willingness can also involve a sense of risk for many people. "There's a little bit of going out on a limb with joy." "When I'm not willing to experience all of life I cut myself off from the experience of joy. I cut myself off when I allow doubt. It's like maybe I won't say the right thing. I experience a little insecurity, a fear. I tell myself this isn't the right thing to say. I stop myself from speaking. I blunt my experience of fear, yet [with fear repressed] I don't experience joy either." Another paradoxically adds, "Here I was experiencing all this sadness, anxiety, negativity. I didn't make these feelings wrong. And I experienced joy. I am astonished. This seemed impossible!" We tend to be judgmental about ourselves when we experience "negative" feelings such as sadness or anxiety. That we can experience joy under these circumstances is seemingly impossible. It does not fit in with our usual way of looking at joy.

With joy there can be a sense of risk, astonishment, a non-rational quality to the experience. "It's almost as though there's a prerequisite of feeling okay about myself before I can be open to experiencing, before I can risk being joyful." "If I'm really being myself, if I'm really experiencing joy, then external situations might fall apart. People may not see it as a joyful experience, they may not understand it. People don't often understand that it's an inner process."

It seems as though gratitude and trust are spiritual qualities that open us to the willingness to experience Self and joy. "We experience joy with other qualities of our inner self, like peace and love. Joy then becomes a way of life." "To be joyful, it's important for me to come from my inner purpose, to trust that purpose rather than the way of the world." In the midst of a tumultuous world, it takes trust and courage to allow our inner self to guide and direct our active participation in life.

What are the gifts which may come through trust in our inner self? "These gifts can be the qualities of our inner self, humility, peace, joy, love, gratitude." "If I am experiencing peace or any other quality of the inner self, the very experience of the inner self is joyful."

"The whole world is brighter. I seem to notice joy in other things as well, that I hadn't noticed before. It is part of the expansiveness that joy is in all things, not just some." "Joy is the most mystical of all experiences that I've ever had, because it is a sense of who I actually am. Being who I am, joy is accompanied by feelings of expansiveness, a feeling of connectedness. Ultimately, joy is trust. It is trust in the timeless and formless." "Joy is a limitless condition that is me."

Dr. H. Spencer Lewis indicated how we can bridge the gap between our reality of a limited self and the experience of limitless joy:

> The real key to happiness, which may be applied for all, is this: Be always considerate of others in all your thoughts, actions, and words. God never intended that man should be unhappy. Happiness is man's birthright, and the only thing which is preventing man from enjoying that birthright is his own blind egotism. Because we are so wrapped up in ourselves, we are failing to enjoy the happiness we should have and hold. We are so proud of our self-styled independence that we have built up a wall of pride around us, through which kindness, joy, consideration, and love cannot penetrate, and it is not until we remove that wall and know that we are of God, and not of ourselves, that true happiness will come to be with us and remain with us now and forevermore.

The following questions are for our personal self-examination, contemplation, and our own exploration of our willingness.

1. At the personal level, when do you experience joy? In relationship and in service for others, when do you experience joy? In experiencing your relationship to the Cosmic, when do you experience joy?

2. Imagine a situation in which you could be experiencing joy. Visualize this situation clearly and in detail. Do you often imagine yourself as joyous? Is joy selfish?

3. What are you doing to promote possibilities for experiencing joy in your life?

4. What are you doing to share joy with others?

5. Experience joy. Experience happiness. Experience self-esteem. Are your experiences the same?

6. Do we require anything in the external world (i.e., an "ability," a "need," a "should," or a "want") in order to experience joy?

7. Are you willing to experience joy?

CHAPTER 12

TRANSCENDENCE

Before transcendence and the consummation of the mystical marriage, there is a letting go of our mistaking form as being essence. In letting go the ultimate importance of outer form, we live in a world of paradox. We go beyond what we thought we needed and lacked, what we thought we should do and failed, what we thought we desired and couldn't have; and going beyond our needs, duties, and desires, we discover that what we are is what we thought we wanted. To abide with such paradox in matters of quality and essence calls upon a supreme trust, courage, and love. Yet, is not the call of our own heart, the voice and direction of our innermost being, not the voice we have longed to hear and join? Ultimately, can there be any other path for us? (Note: again, as with Chapter 11, the following essay was written by George F. Buletza and David M. Aguilera.)

BEYOND WORTHINESS

Exploring what lies beyond worthiness is a challenge. What lies beyond has no words, is undefined, is completely open. We even have difficulty talking about it. Yet, the confidence, the joy, the peace that is experienced as the mystic goes "beyond," makes the seemingly heavy experiences of life more than worth it.

Worthiness is a reality that can color our experience of life. Yet, one of our subjects mysteriously says, "Worthiness, unworthiness? This is a cosmic joke! Worthiness doesn't exist. It's a mental fabrication. It's only a reality." When we are told that our worthiness is a joke, we may feel that the joke is on us. Isn't being worthy important?

A Class Master at the Rosicrucian Order remarks, "I sometimes receive a letter reporting on a student's feelings of unworthiness. The student may feel that he or she hasn't had a psychic experience, or feel guilty about not having incense, or not having an ideal Sanctum. The openness, vulnerability, and warmth these students share with me is very touching. They have heart. Tears come to my eyes when I read these letters from sincere students. I feel sad that these students may believe that these same qualities verify their unworthiness."

As these students' letters point out, a reality of worthiness can be a major issue in the life of a Rosicrucian aspirant. Research subjects indicate, "I thought I was the only one dealing with this issue." "I've always wanted to be worthy, but it's impossible for me." Another subject adds, "I know me. I know my weaknesses. Everything I do isn't good." "I admire those who think they are worthy. I doubt that they really are, though."

How often have we unconsciously said something like this to ourselves? Does worthiness seem to be an ideal that is impossible for us to achieve? Is it something we ought to achieve? "I strive for worthiness. I work hard to earn it, but I'm never actually worthy." "I can't experience what isn't so."

When caught in our reality of unworthiness, our attitudes may be experienced as, " . . . empty, cold, dark, a shell or cave with no way out." " . . . a blackness that's all there is." " . . . a despair that is ultimate and final." " . . . a despair that is a blot on my soul." "I'm doing all the right things, why am I not there yet?" "I do everything I can to serve and become worthy, but it's never enough. I'm still as unworthy as I ever was." "I will never be worthy."

One aspect of this reality can be the idea that others can make us worthy. "Part of me is wanting to be rescued." "There has to be some external source of wisdom that will help me out." "I hunger for someone who will make me right, will see the good qualities in me, make me worthy." "I am in a shell, under a rock, beneath the sea—find me. I want to be loved."

The mental intricacies and convolutions of our realities can be very subtle. "When other people acknowledge me and praise my accomplishments, I feel good. However, the ego craftily intimates, 'That's a lie. You fooled them, too.' Underneath the 'good feeling' I still suspect I'm not worthy." "When I am not worthy, I can't even love myself. Then, I need someone else to show me I'm good enough to be loved again."

In this reality, "There is a sense of burden. Other's expectations and the high ideals of others increase the burden without showing the way out." "This is the ultimate despair, the ultimate impossibility." "Here I am, living out a life of ideals and yet I don't see any worthiness." "Where is the joy!" "Where's the joy that's supposed to be here!"

Our realities, even if they are a fabrication of our mind, can affect the way we perceive and interact with our world. In a recent RCU class, students responded to an exploration of worthiness with, "Help!!!" "Where have you led me with all your damned questions?" "I'm frustrated, confused and hurt, and it's all your fault!" Many of us project the frustration and anger, resulting from our own realities, onto others. This can be an alternative to facing the fear of having a lack within ourselves. "When I feel unworthy, I make judgments, either on myself or on others." "When I judge myself to be evil, bad, awful, there is no willingness to go on, no gratitude." "What joy am I supposed to experience here?"

This reality of unworthiness ultimately brings us to feel that something is fundamentally wrong or lacking in us. In despair, we find this reality of unworthiness is a costly belief. "Cost to me includes lots of stress." "When I feel something is wrong with me, then I feel dissatisfied with everything in my life." "Whatever I do is meaningless." "When I'm trying to cover up that something is wrong with me, then I struggle for an external perfection. I'm not very easy to live with, then." "If I can make the outer world perfect, that would prove that I'm okay." "When I think there's something wrong about me, then I don't acknowledge myself." "I judge myself and have low self-esteem." "I lack spontaneity." "I censor what I say and do." "I don't have anything to contribute." "Everything I've done in the past was a fake." "I never get or give enough love." "I feel numb and weak."

When caught up in a reality of unworthiness we can live out that reality as if it's actually us. "When I succumb to 'knowing' how unworthy I am, my life consists of desperation and despair." "Unworthiness does a number on my solar plexus, like something I've swallowed and it's been sitting there a long time, undigested. I think I want to throw up."

Subjects also report subtle payoffs in maintaining the reality that "something is fundamentally wrong with me." "Then, it's all right to run judgments that I'm better than others or that others are better than me." "If I can convince myself that I'm good, then I don't have to examine that nagging suspicion that I'm not really okay." "I don't risk connection and the experience of oneness." "I get to be free from other people's control." "I get to be in control myself, because if something is wrong with me, then I better stay ahead of the other fellow or he and others will find out!" Other people add, "I don't have to risk getting hurt." "I don't have to risk having a relationship." "I don't risk rejection."

"Secretly, I get to feel I am helpless, hopeless, weak—a victim and a martyr." "It's all right that I work harder to impress others and win approval. With hard work I can return at a new level of mastership. Then people will have to love, honor, and respect me." "I get to work intensely, or I can avoid altogether."

"I don't have to love myself." "I have work to do, responsibilities, obligations. I don't have time to love myself. Besides, that's selfish."

With such costs and payoffs accompanying the reality of unworthiness, how do people experience the reality of worthiness? Is this an improvement? "It doesn't work to be unworthy. I have to be worthy." "My presentation went well. The important points were made. People were so impressed that I made more sales than ever before." "I've wanted this for a long time. The promotion finally came through. I'm a real person." "I just bought a new car. It's really sharp. Silver with gold wheels." "I am a successful businessman. I am proud of my family. I have a beautiful wife. I have two grown and successful children." "I own a house on Hill Crest." "I am satisfied with the respect and importance the community affords my efforts." "Self-esteem is a matter of exercising the proper control over one's emotions and lower nature." "I am a Rosicrucian. Of course, I am worthy. I don't understand people who could think otherwise." "I try very hard to let others know that I, too, am worthy. It takes a lot of effort, but my energy is well spent."

When people are ready to examine the results that even a worthiness reality produces, the surprising result is that the cost and payoff can be much the same as for an unworthiness reality. Problems with stress, perfectionism, relationships, superiority, self-esteem, spiritual oneness, and fulfillment are raised. Is there any genuine benefit in trading one reality for another? Is there another way?

One person exclaims, "No wonder I couldn't get my life to work. Worthiness wasn't it!" "I can finally see that this whole issue is just an ego trip for me." Another person offers the following insight: "Can unworthiness be made worthy? Of course not! We can't be torn between worth and unworthiness for long without feeling crazy. But finally, we touch that inner source of Light, and it's done for us." "Unworthiness seen through its own eyes has no resolution, salvation, hope, for it only sees itself, its own reality. But seen through the eyes of love, we can be healed. After all, worthiness and unworthiness are only realities." In letting go of realities, some members point to, "touching the spiritual," "trusting the Cosmic," "allowing an expansion, a flowering, a blossoming of Self," "experiencing the warmth of a pure heart."

What are we truly seeking, worthiness or the Inner Self? What is most important to us, success or the expression and experience of who we actually are? What comes first, reality or actuality? The Rosicrucian teaches that as a spiritual alchemist we transform our realities, rather than trying to change the actuality of infinite potential, that totality of what we are. The Rosicrucian knows that we can do nothing to actuality. Hence, he works to allow his realities to transmute. He can then experience himself as he is. As one student puts it, "It's the experience of 'I am,' rather than the interpretation or judgment of what I am."

What do people experience when they let go of their reality or belief? "I am free to choose, to create, to experience life in all its possibilities." "I experience Being." "I experience joy." "I experience peace." We can all experience " ... a resting place," " ... a state we all came from and are all returning to, a place called home; a place of peace and no desire; a place that lies within the soul," " ... peace, a state of no effort and no desire, a state of grace."

"Nothing I do can enhance or diminish what I am." "Nothing I do or think or wish or make is necessary to establish my worth. What I am is a gift of the Cosmic." "What I am is the actuality of what is. Realities which deny this

actuality are lies, illusions." "Words do not express the gratitude and the joy . . . ." "In the wholeness of all being, I
rejoice!"

"Isn't it interesting that we find that we are all these
things that we once projected outward, that we thought of
as God?" Certain ancient Greeks spoke of their realization
of God as the *Entheos,* the God Within. David, the psalm-
ist, also spoke of this experience when he prayed, "Bless
Yahweh, my soul."

Through study, self-examination, and personal work,
some Rosicrucian students discover that worthiness is not
what is important to them. However, they can also say that
the exploration of worthiness can lead beyond egocentric
concerns to what is important to them—to an experience of
the God within us all.

The following questions are for our personal self-examination, contemplation, and our own exploration of our
willingness.

1. Is there anything in the external world that can justify
    my worthiness? How much would it take for me to be
    worthy?

2. If I cannot justify my worthiness by actions or posses-
    sions in the outer world, from where might my worthi-
    ness arise? What am I denying if I deny this source of
    my being and worthiness? Is this what I am clearly
    choosing?

3. Are you willing to accept your worthiness as being a
    gift which you cannot justify by deeds and possessions?

4. After being willing to accept the gift of worthiness, are you also willing to let go of it? Are you willing to let go of both worthiness and unworthiness?
5. What is important to you?
6. Are you willing to love yourself?
7. Are you willing to let go of all things of this world, to join, to love all in all circumstances?

When we "let go" of our realities and our need for outer form in our search for meaning, wholeness, and the essence of Self, we come to that transcendent state in which we experience and become aware of the limitless, boundless, and timeless quality of the spiritual. While such a spiritual state can lie at the heart of our deepest "knowing," it can terrify the ego that longs for safety in form. Accepting the experience of the essence of Self without the familiar comfort of form leads the seeker to the most courageous moments of existence.

THROUGH THE ABYSS

This seeker is not a person who is content with ignorance or with questions left unanswered. Hence, the sincere seeker also is willing to probe the mystery of personal existence. An inquiring mind and an impetuous spirit can eventually bring him or her to a great precipice at the limits of ordinary knowledge. Beyond lies the unknown, that realm which most people dare not investigate and thus avoid. Beneath is the appearance of a chasm of darkness. In it lurk the fears and superstitions which people have unconsciously accepted about life, birth, death, immortality, and other mysteries.

What lies beyond the feared "nothingness" of this awesome abyss? Is there any sane reason for Rosicrucian students to carry within them a vision of "the heart unafraid"? Is anything to be gained by a vision of self that the worldly might dismiss as foolhardy? Confronted by our own superstitious beliefs and fears, do we dare disprove them? Are we willing to discover the Great Light hidden behind these beliefs and fears?

To answer these questions, investigators accompanied twenty-two research participants on an inner journey through their own personal abyss. During these exercises, we observed that moving our consciousness through fears and the abyss clears the mind. On the other hand, staying stuck by trying to avoid fear energizes the fear and entraps our consciousness.

By experiencing that fear without judgment or interpretation, and repeatedly questioning, "If this were to happen, then what next?", we keep from getting stuck, and we promote a forward movement which can lead to a rediscovery of Self, and our original intention, purpose, or desire.

To facilitate movement through the abyss each participant began his personal odyssey by attuning with an inner desire, purpose, or intention. For example, one participant realized that his purpose at this time was to learn to trust life. Specifically, he said, "I want to trust that my current relationships are perfect the way they are; I want to trust that the Cosmic will assist me to fulfill my material needs; I want to trust that whatever happens at the seminar I am to present will be the perfect learning experience for me and the attendees."

In his case, we started with his upcoming seminar. "If the seminar isn't successful," we asked, "then what might happen?" He responded with, "I'll look stupid."

"If you were to look stupid, then what?"

"People won't like me," he responded.

"If people don't like you, then what?"

"I'll be alone."

"And then?"

"I'll kill myself."

"And then?"

"I'd have wimped out on life . . . my life would have been worthless and meaningless . . . I'd suffer endless pain . . . I'd be a nothing."

He became "nothing." He experienced how it might be to dwell in a dark abyss of nothingness.

Unexpectedly, he then felt a "profound peace." Experiencing this peace, he wanted to live again. Feeling the vitality of life, he wanted to create. He found himself creating the seminar. Following his fears, he came full circle, returning to the seminar where he started. However, now he knew his fear consisted of meaningless phantoms that could no longer stand in the way of his progress. What is more, he discovered a source of peace within himself.

Another participant wanted to create her first commercial slide show. The financial opportunity was there, but she feared "looking foolish, silly, stupid, commanding no respect." She feared a lack of love, being rejected and alone. If she were rejected and alone, she would die. Imagining death, she only felt a nothingness, a black void.

In order to experience dwelling in this abyss, we asked her to experience this utter nothingness. We asked her, "What do you feel? What is happening?" She began to feel "a profound peace, a peace that passeth understanding." With awe in her voice, she found herself contemplating, creating, being reborn. Reborn, she found herself creating the slide show she originally was afraid to create. By experiencing and deepening her fears, rather than avoiding them, she discovered that her fears looped though an abyss that led to peace, vitality, and creation of the life about which she had only dreamed.

Having passed through her own fear and abyss, another person commented, "In these few minutes I've passed from being unloved, isolated, and alone, to feeling an open heart, new connections with others, and an incredible flood of joy and gratitude."

Some participants came to find a new identity that "actually was always there, only invisible to my old ways of seeing." Others spoke of discovering opportunities that previously they had been afraid to discover. One man recognized how many of his self-indulgences and compulsions were nothing more than ways to avoid confronting his fears. "It's actually my reality, my vision, and my context for perceiving things, that is important to my fulfillment, isn't it?"

"Change my reality and I change my world," said another participant.

Still another described his experience of the abyss as follows: "What my fear would have me believe is that if I were to radiate the sacred light with which I am entrusted, I wouldn't be understood. I'd be excluded, rejected, alone. I'd die. I wouldn't have learned or fulfilled my purpose. I'd be nothing, and I'd never again be given an opportunity to radiate the Light that I am. Pretty stupid!"

With this experience of the looping nature of our fears, this person concluded, "I find that the shadows and the echoes that would fill our minds are always just as stupid and pointless. Yet, we would allow these shadows and echoes to rule our life, to completely determine our behaviors and attitudes in the world, to breed distrust towards loved ones, ourselves, and life. We would allow ourselves to be puppets dancing on the strings of fear, in darkness. But darkness has no substance, and the fears that fill the abyss disappear when the light of consciousness is brought to bear upon them. We pass over the threshold of terror to realize that we are free beings of Light, masters in Self, students evolving as a rose unfolding on a cross of gold."

The experiences of the participants shared in this adventure can be a lesson for all of us. When we choose to express our Mastery in Self, all the terrors and fears we have carried may suddenly seem to strike at us. The Rosicrucian studies tell us that we who possess genuine desire, faith, and perseverance, a "heart unafraid," will choose to enter this personal abyss and will thereby discover Self and realize freedom from fear.

APPENDIX 1

INSIGHT: OBJECT TO SYMBOL

In the Rosicrucian technique of concentration, contemplation, and meditation, insight results as one proceeds from an objective experience to a symbolic experience. In this experiment you will be guided through these various stages by a series of questions. Each question is very specific and designed to draw upon certain mental faculties. Then be as specific as possible with your answers. Answer only the question asked.

After you have become acquainted with the questionnaire, sit in a relaxed, comfortable position and begin to concentrate on an object of interest to you. Any object will work in this experiment. People have had surprising insights with common articles and simple items such as candles, rocks, glasses of water, paper clips, rubber bands, pencils, corks, thumbtacks, and sea shells.

1. How would you objectively describe the object in terms of your five physical senses? What do you see? What does it feel like? What sounds can the object make? Can you smell or taste it?

2. What does the object normally do? What other things can you do with this object? Are there some other things we could do with it or use it for?

3. Now that we know what a thing is and what it will do, the next natural question is how is it able to do what it does? What is it about its form or structure that allows

it to do these things? In other words, what is its mechanism of action? How does it work?

4. Analogously, how are you like the object? Do you do anything in the same way? Do you use a method of doing things similar to this object's method of doing what it does? What is there about you that is like this object? Is this also true of other people? Of humanity? Of the universe?

5. Since we see this method of doing things in ourselves and throughout nature, we must be dealing with more than a mechanism. We must be dealing with a principle or a law of nature. This principle can usually be described in one or two words—e.g., iron might symbolize strength or weakness; a pencil might symbolize communication; etc. What does this object symbolize to you?

6. We have described the principle represented by this object in a word or two. But if you met someone from another country who did not speak your language, how would you describe or convey this principle to him? Since most people can communicate with pictures, what picture comes to mind as you experience or understand the principle? What picture would describe the meaning of this principle to you?

7. Choose one symbol from your picture. Now, imagine what it would be like to become that symbol. Up to now, notice how you have been looking at the images in your mind as through they are apart from you. Let us now shift perspective and imagine what it might be

like if you become one of the things in your picture. Just release and let the experience and the surprises happen.

When your imaginative experience is completed, think back over your experience and answer the following:

1. Describe your experience. Objectively, what happened? Subjectively, what were your feelings?

2. Did you have any major insights about the object of your meditation?

3. What have you learned about yourself? About others? About the universe?

4. Did you feel any shift of consciousness as you progressed from one question to the next? Can you associate specific questions with the states of consciousness called *concentration, contemplation,* and *meditation?*

5. What questions were the easiest? Hardest? What might this tell you about yourself?

6. Does the process as outlined in this experiment have any importance or special meaning to you? Are there any practical implications for using this process in other areas of your life?

INSIGHT:
SYMBOL INTERPRETATION

In the first experiment we were able to reach insight through what is called *inductive thinking*. It moves from an objective reality to a symbolic reality. However, it is also possible to experience insight by reversing this process, i.e., proceeding from a symbolic reality to an objective reality. This *deductive* approach is helpful in understanding works of art, dreams, and symbols received in meditation.

In this experiment you will again be guided through various states of consciousness by a series of questions. Each question is very specific and designed to draw upon certain mental faculties. Be as specific as possible with your answers. Answer only the question asked.

After reading the entire questionnaire, sit in a relaxed, comfortable position. Choose a symbol from a dream, a meditation, or from any illustration or picture.

1.   Choose one symbol to work with. Now imagine what it would be like to become that symbol. Ask yourself what you might experience if you were the symbol. Relax, visualize, be receptive. Do not "control" or analyze your visualization once it is formed, but simply observe what happens.

2.   When your imaginative experience is completed, think back over your experience and then describe it. Ob-

jectively, what happened? Subjectively, what were your feelings?

3. Using one or two words, describe the natural law or principle which your symbol and experience represent. For example, a symbol might represent strength, change, communication, etc.

4. Does this principle manifest in nature? Does humanity reflect this principle? Do you in your life manifest this principle?

5. What is it about you that lets you reflect or manifest this principle? How are you able to do this? What is there about you that lets you function in this way?

6. You have identified the method or process by which you and others are able to manifest this principle. What are some other ways in which this process or method can be used?

7. Having experienced this principle and having discovered *how* you manifest this principle in your life, do you see some specific ways you might use this information to reach some goals in you life? Does this insight give greater meaning to some areas of your life? Do you look at your life and the world differently than you did before?

When your experience is completed, think back over your experience and answer the following:

1. Did you have any major insights during this experience?

2. What did you learn about yourself? About others? About the universe?

3. Did you feel any shift in consciousness as you progressed from one question to another? Can you associate specific questions with the states of consciousness called *concentration, contemplation,* and *meditation?*

4. What questions were the hardest for you? The easiest? What might this tell you about yourself?

5. How would you compare this experience with the previous one? Which was easier for you? What might this tell you about yourself?

6. Does the process as outlined in this experiment have any importance or special meaning to you? Are there any practical implications for using this process in other areas of your life?

THE CLUSTER PROCESS

1. Put the seed idea in a circle at the center of a page.

2. Let word associations, images, and feelings radiate outward from the center like an unfolding flower. Circle each of your associations and connect each circle with lines to the seed idea at the center.

3. If one association leads to another, then another, and then another, just follow them through, connecting associated circles . . . ideas . . . with lines.

4. When a meaningful pattern arising from your cluster dawns upon you, write a short vignette or "thumbnail" description.

5. Finally, write a brief record of your overall experience with the Cluster Process. Keep this record, look it over occasionally so that you can see what you are continuing to learn from the process.

After you have done clustering on several occasions you may wish to compare your records. This will help you gain insights into your own creative way of thinking.

Every time you use the Cluster Process you can move another step closer to knowing yourself.

REFERENCE NOTES AND BIBLIOGRAPHY

CHAPTER 2

Source:

Bukay, M. & Buletza, G. (1977) Mindquest: The insight experience. Create your own symbols of transformation. *Rosicrucian Digest* LV(2):31.

CHAPTER 3

Footnotes:

[1]Globus, G., Maxwell, G., & Savodnik, I., eds. (1976) *Consciousness and the Brain,* Plenum Press, N.Y.; Ferguson, M. (1978) Karl Pribram's changing reality. *Human Behavior* 7(5):28; Ferguson, M. (1977) A new perspective on reality. *Brain/Mind Bulletin* 2(16):1-4; Lashley, K.S. (1950) In search of the engram, in: *Physiological Mechanisms in Animal Behavior,* Academic Press, NY, p. 454; Pribram, K. (1971) *Languages of the Brain,* Brooks/Cole Publ. Co., Monterey, CA, p. 140; Shaw, R.E. & Bransford, J., eds. (1977) *Perceiving, Acting and Knowing,* Erlbaum/John Wiley, NY.

[2]Batin, T., ed. (1971) *Quantum Theory and Beyond,* Cambridge University Press, Cambridge; Bentov, I. (1977) *Stalking the Wild Pendulum,* E.P. Dutton, NY; Bohm, D. & Hiley, B. (1975) On the intuitive understanding of nonlocality as implied by quantum theory. *Foundations of Physics* 5:93.

Sources:

Buletza, G. (1977) Mindquest: Rosicrucians thinking together I. *Rosicrucian Digest* LV (2):15.

Buletza, G., Bukay, M., & Schaa, J. (1978) Mindquest: Rosicrucians thinking together II. What is thought? *Rosicrucian Digest* LVI(7):16.

Buletza, G., Bukay, M., & Schaa J. (1978) Mindquest: Rosicrucians thinking together III. The images of man. *Rosicrucian Digest* LVI(8):22.

Buletza, G., Bukay, M., & Schaa J. (1978) Mindquest: Rosicrucians thinking together IV. The hidden meaning within thought. *Rosicrucian Digest* LVI(9):22.

CHAPTER 4

Sources:
Buletza, G. (1983) Mindquest: Rosicrucians thinking together: On the nature of confidence. *Rosicrucian Digest.* 61(8):22.

Buletza, G. & Huff, S. (1984) Mindquest: Confidence, the experience. *Rosicrucian Digest* 62(9):19.

Buletza, G. & Huff, S. (1984) Mindquest: Attaining confidence. *Rosicrucian Digest.* 62(10):20.

Buletza, G. & Huff, S. (1984) Mindquest: Confidence, the manifestation. *Rosicrucian Digest.* 62(11):11.

CHAPTER 6

For further reading:
Bonelli, M.L.R. & Shea, W.R. eds. (1975). *Reason, Experiment & Mysticism in the Scientific Revolution,* Neale Watson Academic Publ., New York.

Bronowski, J. *Science & Human Values,* Harper & Row, New York.

Bunge, M. (1962) *Intuition & Science,* Prentice Hall, New Jersey.

Einstein, A. (1950) *Out of My Later Years,* Philosophical Library, New York.

Kuhn, T.S. (1970) *The Structure of Scientific Revolutions,* 2nd ed., University of Chicago Press, Chicago.

Silberer, H. (1951) Report of a method of eliciting and observing certain symbolic hallucination phenomena, in: *The Organization and Pathology of Thought,* ed. by D. Rapaport, Columbia Univ. Press, New York.

Sinnoi, E. (1957) *Matter, Mind & Man,* Harper & Row, New York.

Source:

Buletza, G., Allen, M., Bukay, M., & Schaa, J. (1978) Mindquest: The science of intuition. *Rosicrucian Digest* LVI(6):18.

CHAPTER 7

Footnotes:

[1]AMORC members may wish to review the monographs of the Third Temple Degree.

[2]*Rosicrucian Manual* (1918; revised 1978) AMORC, San Jose, CA, pp. 170 &176.

[3]*Ibid.,* p. 152.

[4]Bettelheim, B. (1977) *The Uses of Enchantment: The Meaning & Importance of Fairy Tales,* Vantage Books, New York.

[5]Spiegelman, J.M. (1974) *The Tree: tales in psycho-mythology,* Phoenix House, Inc. Publishers, Los Angeles.

[6]Storm, Hyemeyohsts (1972) *Seven Arrows,* Ballantine Books, New York.

[7]Buletza, G. (1977) Mindquest: Rosicrucians Thinking Together, A New Experiment, *Rosicrucian Digest,* February, pp. 15-19.

[8]Neihardt, J.G. (1961) *Black Elk Speaks,* University of Nebraska Press, Lincoln, NB.

For further reading:

Arnheim, R. (1972) *Visual Thinking,* University of California Press, Berkeley, CA.

Dubois, P.E. (1977) Interview: Athletes in the rat race, *Human Behavior* 6 (3):38.

Fessier, M. (1976) Transcendental running, *Human Behavior* 5 (7):16-20.

Gallwey, W.T. (1974) *The Inner Game of Tennis,* Random House, New York.

Gallwey, W.T. (1976) *Inner Tennis: Playing the Game,* Random House, New York.

Ghiselin, B. (ed. 1952) *The Creative Process,* University of California Press, Berkeley, CA.

Horowitz, M. (1970) *Image Formation and Cognition,* Appleton-Century-Crofts, New York.

Ismail, A.H. & Trachtman, L.E. (1973) Jogging the imagination, *Psychology Today,* 6 (10):79.

Jacobson, E. (1965) *How to Relax and Have Your Baby,* McGraw Hill, New York.

Jacobson, E. (1938) *Progressive Relaxation,* University of Chicago Press, Chicago.

Klinger, E. (1971) *Structure and Functions of Fantasy,* Wiley-Interscience, New York.

Koestler, A. (1964) *The Act of Creation,* MacMillan Company, New York.

Maltz, M. (1966) *Psycho-Cybernetics,* Pocket Books, New York.

May, R. (1975) *The Courage to Create,* W.W. Norton & Co., New York.

McKim, R. (1972) *Experiences in Creative Thinking,* Brooks/Cole Publ. Co., Monterey, CA.

Oglivie, B.C. & Tutko, T.A. (1971) If you want to build character, try something else, *Psychology Today,* October.

Richardson, A. (1969) *Mental Imagery,* Springer Publ., New York.

Rosner, S. & Abt, L.E. (1970) *The Creative Experience,* Grossman Publ., New York.

Rugg, S. (1963) *Imagination,* Harper & Row, New York.

Samuels, M. & Samuels, N. (1975) *Seeing With the Mind's Eye,* Random House/Bookwords, New York and San Francisco.

Segal, S.J. (1971) *The Adaptive Function of Imagery,* Academic Press, New York.

Sheeham, P. (ed. 1972) *The Function and Nature of Imagery,* Academic Press, New York.

Spino, M. (1976) *Beyond Jogging: The Inner Spaces of Running,* Celestial Arts Publ. Co., Millbrae, CA.

Williams, R.L. & Youssel, Z.I. (1971) Tie Line, *Psychology Today,* October.

Sources:
Schaa, J. (1980) Mindquest: Imagination: The inward dream of the soul. *Rosicrucian Digest* 58(2):20.

Bukay, M. (1977) The circle: American Indian guide to personal understanding. *Rosicrucian Digest.* LV(6):8.

Buletza, G. (1977) Mindquest: "Exercising" the imagination. *Rosicrucian Digest.* LV(5):22.

CHAPTER 8
Footnotes:
[1]Rico, G.L. (1983) *Writing the Natural Way (Using right brain techniques to relate your expressive powers),* J.P. Tarcher, Los Angeles.

[2]Buzan, T. (1974) *Use Both Sides of Your Brain (New techniques to help you read efficiently, study effectively, solve problems, remember more, think creatively),* E.P. Dutton & Co., New York.

[3]Buletza, G. (1983) Are You A Walking Question Mark:?, *Rosicrucian Digest* 61(11):33.

[4]Franz, M.L. von (1970) *Apuleius' Golden Ass,* Spring Publications, Zurich, Switzerland.

[5]Brown, B., Whitten, R. (1982) Behavioral Dramas Life Training Seminar, Kieros Foundation, San Jose, CA.

For further reading:

Linden, W. (1973) Practicing of meditation by school children and their levels of field independence-dependence, test anxiety and reading achievement, *Journal of Counseling and Clinical Psychology* 41:139-143.

Schwartz, G.E. (1974) Meditation as an altered trait of consciousness: Current findings on stress reactivity and creativity. *American Psychological Association 82nd Annual Meeting,* New Orleans.

CHAPTER 9

Footnote:

[1]Andrea, R. (1990) *The Mystic Path,* Rosicrucian Order, AMORC., pp. 27-28.

Sources:

Buletza, G. (1983) Mindquest: Evoking your creative power. *Rosicrucian Digest.* 61(11):22.

Buletza, G. (1983) Healing the whole person. *Rosicrucian Digest.* 61(7):10.

Buletza, G. (1977) Mindquest: Creative expression: a marriage of the mind. *Rosicrucian Digest* LV(6):17

Buletza, G. Buletza & Conrod, J.L. (1983) Mindquest: Clustering for change. *Rosicrucian Digest* 61(12):22.

Buletza, G. (1985) Mindquest: Clustering for enlightenment. *Rosicrucian Digest.* 63(7):21.

CHAPTER 10

Footnote:

[1]Jung, C.G. (1953) *Collected Works. Psychology and Alchemy,* Vol. 12. Pantheon Books Inc., New York. p. 140.

Source:
Taken from an extemporaneous lecture delivered in AMORC's Supreme Temple on March 18, 1986, by George F. Buletza.

CHAPTER 11
Sources:
Buletza, G. & Aguilera, D.M. (1987) Mindquest: Willingness to be ourselves. *Rosicrucian Digest.* 65(2):21.

Buletza, G. & Aguilera, D.M. (1987) Mindquest: Gratitude. *Rosicrucian Digest.* 65(3):23.

CHAPTER 12
Sources:
Buletza, G. & Aguilera, D.M. (1987) Mindquest: Beyond Worthiness. *Rosicrucian Digest.* 65(4)28.

Buletza, G. (1986) Mindquest: Through the abyss. *Rosicrucian Digest.* 64(1):24.

THE ROSICRUCIAN ORDER
Purpose and Work of the Order

Anticipating questions which may be asked by the readers of this book, the publishers take this opportunity to explain the purpose of the Order and how you may learn more about it.

There is only one universal Rosicrucian Order existing in the world today, united in its various jurisdictions, and having one Supreme Council in accordance with the original plan of the ancient Rosicrucian manifestoes. The Rosicrucian Order is not a religious or sectarian society.

This international organization retains the ancient traditions, teachings, principles, and practical helpfulness of the Order as founded centuries ago. It is known as the *Ancient Mystical Order Rosae Crucis,* which name, for popular use, is abbreviated into AMORC. The headquarters of the English Grand Lodge, AMORC, is located at San Jose, California.

The Order is primarily a humanitarian movement, making for greater health, happiness, and peace in people's *earthly lives,* for we are not concerned with any doctrine devoted to the interests of individuals living in an unknown, future state. The Work of Rosicrucians is to be done *here* and *now*; not that we have neither hope nor expectation of *another* life after this, but we *know* that the happiness of the future depends upon *what we do today for others* as well as for ourselves.

Secondly, our purposes are to enable all people to live harmonious, productive lives, as Nature intended, enjoying *all* the privileges of Nature and all benefits and gifts equally with all of humanity; and to be *free* from the shackles of superstition, the limits of ignorance, and the sufferings of avoidable *Karma.*

The Work of the Order, using the word "work" in an official sense, consists of teaching, studying, and testing such laws of God and Nature as make our members Masters in the Holy Temple (the physical body), and Workers in the Divine Laboratory (Nature's domains). This is to enable our members to render *more efficient help* to those who do not know, and who need or require help and assistance.

Therefore, the Order is a school, a college, a fraternity, with a laboratory. The members are students and workers. The graduates are unselfish servants of God to humanity, efficiently educated, trained, and experienced, attuned with the mighty forces of the Cosmic or Divine Mind, and Masters of matter, space, and time. This makes them essentially Mystics, Adepts, and Magi—creators of their own destiny. There are no other benefits or rights. All members are pledged to give unselfish service, without other hope or expectation of remuneration than to evolve the Self and prepare for a *greater* Work.

The Rosicrucian Sanctum membership program offers a means of personal home study. Instructions are sent regularly in specially prepared weekly lectures and lessons, and contain a summary of the Rosicrucian principles with such a wealth of personal experiments, exercises, and tests as will make each member highly proficient in the attainment of certain degrees of mastership. These correspondence lessons and lectures comprise several Degrees. Each Degree has its own Initiation ritual, to be performed by the member at home in his or her private home sanctum. Such rituals are not the elaborate rituals used in the Lodge Temples, but are simple and of practical benefit to the student.

If you are interested in knowing more of the history and present-day helpful offerings of the Rosicrucians, you may receive a *free* copy of the introductory booklet entitled the *Mastery of Life* by calling our toll-free telephone number 1-800-88-AMORC, or by writing to:

Rosicrucian Order, AMORC
1342 Naglee Avenue
San Jose, California 95191, U.S.A.

ROSICRUCIAN LIBRARY

SELF MASTERY AND FATE WITH THE
CYCLES OF LIFE
by H. Spencer Lewis, Ph.D., F.R.C.

This book demonstrates how to harmonize the self with the cyclic forces of each life.

Happiness, health, and prosperity are available for those who know the periods in their own life that enhance the success of varying activities. Eliminate "chance" and "luck," cast aside "fate," and replace these with self mastery. Complete with diagrams and lists of cycles.

THE MYSTICAL LIFE OF JESUS
by H. Spencer Lewis, Ph.D., F.R.C.

A full account of Jesus' life, containing the story of his activities in the periods not mentioned in the Gospel accounts, *reveals the real Jesus* at last.

This book required a visit to Palestine and Egypt to secure verification of the strange facts found in Rosicrucian records. Its revelations, predating the discovery of the Dead Sea Scrolls, show aspects of the Essenes unavailable elsewhere.

This volume contains many mystical symbols (fully explained), photographs, and an unusual portrait of Jesus.

SO MOTE IT BE!
by Christian Bernard, F.R.C.

Explore Rosicrucian views on themes of spirituality and philosophy with Imperator Christian Bernard, whose life has been steeped in the philosophy, heritage, and tradition of AMORC. Each chapter covers a topic near and dear to the soul of students of mysticism, including: the power of universal love, the heritage of the Rose-Croix, fear of death, the obscure night, free will, reincarnation, the definition and practice of mystical initiation, and other fascinating topics.

SEPHER YEZIRAH—A BOOK ON CREATION
or The Jewish Metaphysics of Remote Antiquity
by Dr. Isidor Kalisch, Translator

The ancient basis for Qabalistic thought is revealed in this outstanding metaphysical essay concerning all creation. It explains the secret name of Jehovah.

Containing both the Hebrew and English texts, its sixty-one pages have been photolithographed from the 1877 edition. As an added convenience to students of Qabalah, it contains a glossary of the original Hebraic words and terms.

SECRET SYMBOLS OF THE ROSICRUCIANS
of the 16th and 17th Centuries

This large book is a rare collection of full-size plates of original Rosicrucian symbols and documents. A cherished possession for students of mysticism, this collection includes the Hermetic, alchemical, and spiritual meaning of the unique Rosicrucian symbols and philosophical principles passed down through the ages.

The plates are from originals and are rich in detail. The book is 12" by 18" and is bound in durable textured cover stock.

ROSICRUCIAN PRINCIPLES FOR THE
HOME AND BUSINESS
by H. Spencer Lewis, Ph.D., F.R.C.

This volume contains the practical application of Rosicrucian teachings to such problems as: ill health, common ailments, how to increase one's income or promote business propositions. It shows not only what to do, but what to avoid, in using metaphysical and mystical principles in starting and bringing into realization new plans and ideas.

Both business organizations and business authorities have endorsed this book.

THE INNER WORLD OF DREAMS
by Phyllis L. Pipitone, Ph.D., F.R.C.

Learn all about your dreams and what they can teach you about yourself and your world. The author takes the reader on a fascinating voyage into a mysterious world in which the dramas of the night can range from the completely outrageous to the lofty and sublime. *The Inner World of Dreams* is written in an easy-to-read style for the beginning and intermediate explorer of the world of dreams. It will give you a good start towards increased insight into your dreams.

LEMURIA—THE LOST CONTINENT OF THE PACIFIC
by Wishar S. Cervé

Where the Pacific now rolls in a majestic sweep for two thousand miles, there was once a vast continent known as Lemuria.

The scientific evidences of this lost race and its astounding civilization with the story of the descendants of the survivors present a cyclical viewpoint of rise and fall in the progress of civilization.

"UNTO THEE I GRANT . . ."
as revised by Sri Ramatherio

Out of the mysteries of the past comes this antique book that was written two thousand years ago, but was hidden in manuscript form from the eyes of the world and given only to the Initiates of the temples in Tibet to study privately.

It can be compared only with the writings attributed to Solomon in the Bible of today. It deals with human passions, weaknesses, fortitudes, and hopes. Included is the story of the expedition into Tibet that secured the manuscript and the Grand Lama's permission to translate it.

MENTAL ALCHEMY
by Ralph M. Lewis, F.R.C.

We can transmute our problems to workable solutions through *mental alchemy*. While this process is neither easy nor instantaneously effective, eventually the serious person will be rewarded. Certain aspects of our lives *can* be altered to make them more compatible with our goals.

Use this book to alter the direction of your life through proper thought and an understanding of practical mystical philosophy.

THE SECRET DOCTRINES OF JESUS
by H. Spencer Lewis, Ph.D., F.R.C.

Even though the sacred writings of the Bible have had their contents scrutinized, judged, and segments removed by twenty ecclesiastical councils since the year A.D. 328, there still remain buried in unexplained passages and parables the Great Master's *personal* doctrines. Every thinker will find *hidden truths* in this book.

MANSIONS OF THE SOUL
by H. Spencer Lewis, Ph.D., F.R.C.

Reincarnation—the world's most disputed doctrine! What did Jesus mean when he referred to the "mansions in my Father's house"?

This book demonstrates what Jesus and his immediate followers knew about the rebirth of the soul, as well as what has been taught by sacred works and scholarly authorities in all parts of the world.

Learn about the cycles of the soul's reincarnations and how you can become acquainted with your present self and your past lives.

ORDER BOOKS FROM:
ALEXANDRIA CATALOG SALES
1-888-767-2278
Rosicrucian Order, AMORC, 1342 Naglee Avenue
San Jose, California 95191, U.S.A.

For a complete, illustrated catalog and price list of the books listed herein, please call or write to the address listed above.